Serge

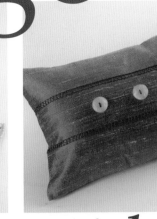

with confidence

Nancy Zieman

©2006 by Nancy Zieman

Published by

kp books
An Imprint of F+W Publications

700 East State Street • Iola, WI 54990-0001
715-445-2214 • 888-457-2873

Our toll-free number to place an order or obtain
a free catalog is (800) 258-0929.

Library of Congress Catalog Number: 2005934239

ISBN 13-digit: 978-0-87349-855-5
ISBN 10-digit: 0-87349-855-0

Edited by Maria L. Turner
Illustrated by Laure Noe
Photographs by Dale Hall and Keith Glasgow
Nancy's Notions editorial staff: Pat Hahn and Diane Dhein

Printed in China

13 12 11   10 9 8

Table of Contents

Lettuce Edge

chapter 1

Serger Quest

A serger may be compact, but don't let that fool you. This specialty machine stitches up to 1,500 stitches per minute, trims the seam and overcasts the edge at the same time! The serger's popularity has spread so fast that you needn't go on a quest to find one. Sergers are available from just about every major sewing machine company.

What is a Serger?

- A serger is a compact machine that uses loopers instead of a bobbin.

- Sergers stitch the seam, trim the excess seam allowance and overcast the edge all in one operation. This process gives you professional-looking garments and crafts in a fraction of the time it would take to complete them using a conventional sewing machine.

- Most sergers stitch at speeds between 1,300 and 1,500 stitches per minute. That's twice the speed of a conventional sewing machine, which stitches between 600 and 1,000 stitches per minute.

Who Needs a Serger?

- Anyone who sews and wants projects to look professional. A serger easily finishes seams and hems.

- Those who sew a lot of knit fabrics. A serger stitches knit seams without stretching them out of shape.

- People who want to venture into new design capabilities without using decorative stitches or embroidery. A serger performs stitch variations and is able to utilize decorative threads.

- Sewers who want to finish sewing projects fast and efficiently. A serger stitches at twice the speed of a conventional machine.

Note from Nancy

Keep in mind that a serger will not replace your sewing machine. It complements your sewing machine with enhanced speed, neatness and creativity. From eliminating raveling seams to creating easy embellishments, a serger is definitely worth considering!

Selecting a Serger

Ask yourself these questions:

? *How will I use the serger?*
Sergers can have a wide variety of stitches and attachments, so it is a good idea to know how you plan to use the machine. If you are merely planning to finish seams, a simple 3/4-thread machine is probably all you need. However, if you plan to cover stitch hems, as in ready-to-wear and want the latest in decorative features, consider a serger that offers a bit more.

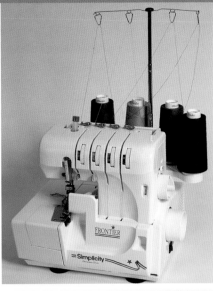

? *What features are important?*
Check out the available features and decide how often you would use them to determine if they would be beneficial.

? *Which types of sergers are available for purchase?*
Most companies offer several different models. These are the six most common types:
- 3/4-Thread Overlock
- 2/3/4-Thread Overlock
- 2/3/4/5-Thread Overlock
- Overlock/Coverlock/Chain Stitch Combination
- Overlock/Coverlock/Chain Stitch with Deco Cover Thread Attachment
- Coverlock/Chain Stitch

? *What kind of support will the dealer and manufacturer offer?*
Knowing you have a network that can provide information and inspiration is a definite "plus." Look for:
- Knowledgeable sales staff who can answer questions quickly and informatively
- An on-site repair technician
- An active club or support group to help you learn more about your machine

? *Do I receive free lessons?*
Lessons are a must! If you have never sewn on a serger before, you not only need to learn how to thread it, but also some basic maneuvering skills.

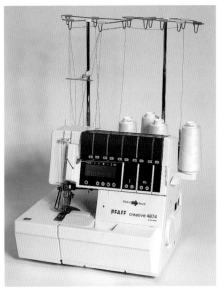

? *What price range am I considering?*
The amount you spend will be determined by the machine's features. The price of any serger increases with the stitch capabilities and exclusive features such as automatic needle threaders, Jet-Air Threading™, ease of tension control, decorative stitching, etc.

Anatomy of a Serger

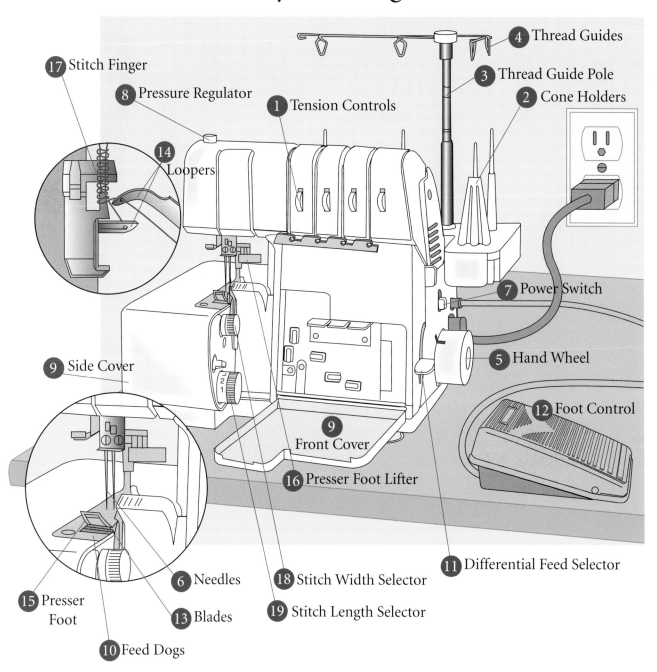

17 Stitch Finger

8 Pressure Regulator

1 Tension Controls

4 Thread Guides

3 Thread Guide Pole

2 Cone Holders

14 Loopers

7 Power Switch

9 Side Cover

5 Hand Wheel

12 Foot Control

9 Front Cover

16 Presser Foot Lifter

11 Differential Feed Selector

6 Needles

18 Stitch Width Selector

15 Presser Foot

13 Blades

19 Stitch Length Selector

10 Feed Dogs

Note from Nancy

Your serger may not look exactly like the one shown above, but it will have similar components. Check your instruction manual to see where these parts are located on your machine.

1. **Tension Controls** determine how fast and how much thread is dispersed at a time to achieve a balanced stitch.

2. **Cone Holders** position cones of thread and keep them from moving as the thread unwinds.

3. **Thread Guide Pole or Thread Antenna** holds the first thread guides. These first guides keep the thread up and away from the spool to prevent tangling. The thread antenna should always be raised completely when serging.

4. **Thread Guides** hold the thread on its way to the needle or looper to produce an evenly formed stitch.

5. **Hand Wheel** moves the needles and loopers so they can form a stitch. The wheel moves by itself when you press the foot pedal or it can be moved manually to take a few test stitches. Always turn the hand wheel toward you unless your instructions specify otherwise.

6. **Needles** are necessary to form a stitch. One to five needles may be used, depending on the model and stitch. The needle thread holds the looper threads together, so at least one needle is always used.

7. **Power Switch** controls the light and power to the machine and is usually located on the lower right side of the serger.

8. **Pressure Regulator** (available on select models) controls the amount of pressure the presser foot exerts on the fabric. Too much pressure stretches the fabric. Too little pressure allows the fabric to slip too easily under the presser foot.

9. **Front and Side Covers** (opening side cover available on select models) allow access to the loopers for threading and aid in removing built-up lint and serger trimmings.

10. **Feed Dogs** are teeth-like grippers in the throat plate that move the fabric through the machine. Some sergers have a double set of feed dogs that allow fabric to feed faster or slower from front to back; they can be adjusted with the Differential Feed Selector.

11. **Differential Feed Selector** (available on select models) controls how the feed dogs grab the fabric. It allows each set of feed dogs to move at a different rate of speed. The differential feed ratio is usually adjustable from .05 to 2.25.

12. **Foot Control** determines the speed at which the machine serges. Cords from the foot control connect to both the machine and an electrical outlet.

13. **Blades** (stationary and moving—sometimes called "knives") trim the fabric. The moving blade cuts the fabric in conjunction with the stationary blade. The moving blade is usually the first blade that needs to be changed.

14. **Loopers** work much like little knitting needles. The lower looper finishes the back of the seam, the upper looper finishes the front of the seam and the needle threads hold the two together. Some machines also have a chain looper, not shown.

15. **Presser Foot** attaches to the presser bar and holds the fabric in place during serging.

16. **Presser Foot Lifter** raises the presser foot up and down to secure and release the fabric during stitching.

17. **Stitch Finger** extends from the throat plate or on some machines, from the presser foot. The stitches are formed over the stitch finger.

18. **Stitch Width Selector** determines the height of the stitch that surrounds the seam edge.

19. **Stitch Length Selector** determines the length of individual stitches.

Extra Features

- **Jet-Air Threading**™ is a unique threading system exclusive to some Baby Lock® sergers. Merely position the looper threads in the threading ports and press the threading lever inside the front cover to automatically thread the loopers.

- **Tubular Loopers** are a patented system of narrow tubes through which the upper and lower looper threads travel during Jet-Air Threading™ on certain Baby Lock® sergers. There are no lower thread guides to follow and no exposed threads to tangle, so this machine can be threaded in any order.

- **ATD (Automatic Thread Delivery) or ATS (Automatic Tension System)** eliminates tension controls; measures and releases just the right amount of thread to achieve a balanced stitch.

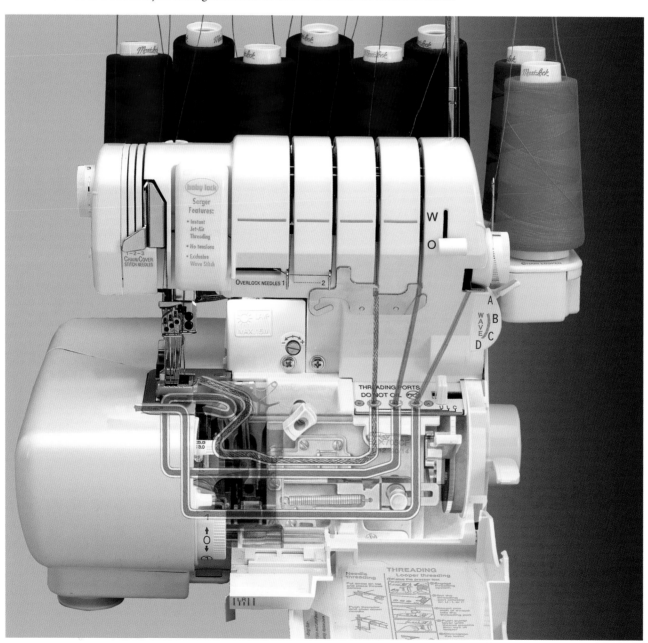

Photo courtesy of Baby Lock®

- **Color-Coded Threading** makes it easier to thread the looper and needle thread paths.

- **Free Arm** allows you to serge with ease in tight places, like cuffs and collars.

- **Pro Cards** are compatible software cards that have three preprogrammed stitches and three blank spaces for programming favorite settings. Machines that use Pro Cards can accept machine updates via these cards.

- **Thread Cutters** are built-in and usually located on the serger's left side above the presser foot. They allow you to cut thread tails after completing stitching.

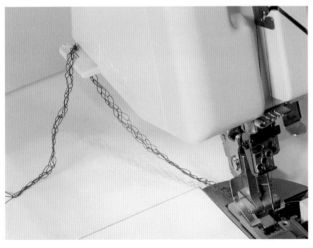

- **Automatic Needle Threader** threads the needle at the touch of a lever.

- **Electronic Speed Reducer** is a "Serger Policeman" that allows you to set the serger speed. It is especially helpful when you are first learning your machine and when you have children who will be serging.

- **Tilting Needle Clamp** makes changing the needles a snap.

- **Rotary Hook for Chain Looper** (exclusive to Pfaff) guarantees quiet and vibration-free serging.

- **Informational LCD Screen** shows pertinent information for a selected stitch. On some machines, you can choose different languages, change settings for a stitch and save settings to the machine's memory.

- **Decorative Stitches** allow you to couch threads and yarns in place for unlimited effects.

- **Built-In Light** is included on most sergers to increase visibility. The most popular type is the tru-color light, which is energy efficient, reduces eye strain and simulates natural light.

- **Waste Tray** keeps your serger trimmings at bay and your countertop clean. Remove tray to empty it.

Thread Know-How

Keep in mind that you won't need as many colors of serger thread as sewing thread, but you will need more cones of each color. You will generally need four to five cones of each color, depending on which serger you have. Black, white, cream and gray are the basics. They blend with just about any color fabric for inside seams. You may want to have some speciality threads on hand for decorative serging.

Before you thread your machine, let's take a look at few different types of thread you will be using along your serging journey.

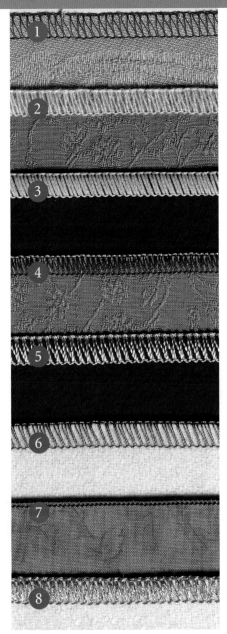

Types of Thread for Serging

Two-ply polyester cone thread is the most popular for all-purpose serging. It's usually cross-wound and winds off the top of the spool better for high-speed sewing. It is lightweight, so seams will be soft. Because several threads are used on each seam, it is best to use a two-ply versus a three-ply thread so seams won't be so bulky.

Note from Nancy

There are many brands of polyester cone thread. Take a 12" length and look closely at it. If it contains many short fibers, it might not be the best thread choice, as it will develop a lot of lint as you serge and probably won't be as strong.

The following threads, although not all-inclusive, are some of the most popular specialty serger threads:

1. **Cotton-Wrapped Polyester Thread** is strong and elastic. The cotton coating adds heat resistance and helps it blend with natural fiber fabrics.

2. **Serging Yarn** is developed specifically for a serger. It is cross-wound and great for finishing edges on blankets or garments made for warmth and durability.

3. **Texturized Nylon Thread,** such as Woolly Nylon, provides extra coverage. When you pull a length of texturized nylon thread, it gets thinner; when you let it relax, it puffs up and is thicker. The tension causes it to stretch and look like regular thread as you stitch. When the stitches are released, they fill in.

4. **Fusible Thread** is a heat-activated thread that fuses when pressed with a steam iron. Use this thread in your serger's lower looper.

5. **Pearl Crown Rayon Thread** gives a nice luster to your stitches. That luster makes the thread slippery. Use a thread net to keep the thread from "pooling," getting caught up in your cone holder or twisting together.

6. **Sulky 12 wt. Cotton or Jean Stitch Cotton Thread** are attractive for decorative serging where you need a stable thread that is a little heavier than regular cone thread.

7. **Rayon Embroidery Thread** is a lustrous thread used for rolled edges and decorative serging on fine fabrics.

8. **Metallic Thread** is used mainly in the loopers. Finer metallic threads can be combined to give a heavier look to serging.

Thread Storage

Store serger thread in drawers, baskets, racks or wherever it is convenient for you within your sewing area. Protect thread from dust by keeping it covered, if possible. Two of the most common ways to store serger cone thread are on cone racks and pegboard.

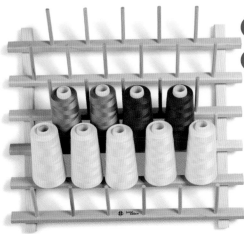

Helpful Tools and Supplies

Basic Supplies

These helpful tools are usually included with a serger. You will find them invaluable to your serging success.

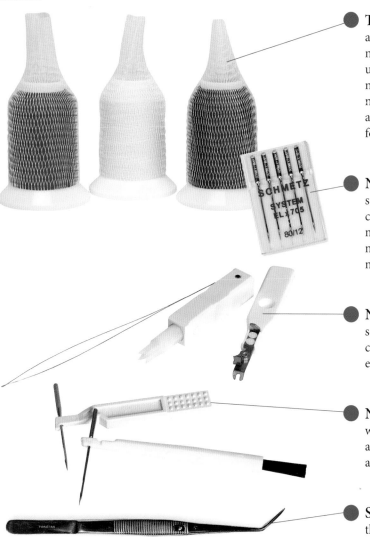

Thread Nets protect the thread from pooling and getting caught as you are stitching. Thread nets come in many different lengths and are usually a soft polyester netting. Cut your thread net a few inches longer than the spool. Insert the net in the hole at the bottom of the thread cone and bring the remainder up over the spool to form a little thread basket.

Needles best suited for your serger are suggested in your owner's manual. Many sergers can use regular sewing machine needles, but most of the cover stitch models require a special needle. It is very important to use the suggested needle size to get well-formed stitches.

Needle Threaders are built-in on some sergers. With others, you can purchase commercially made threaders to make threading easier.

Needle Inserters not only hold the needle with the flat side in the correct direction, but also align the needle into the proper position and hold it until you tighten the screw.

Serger Tweezers are invaluable for threading the loopers or holding your needle while inserting it if you don't have a needle inserter. With luck, you won't have to use the tweezers to retrieve a needle or some other object from inside the serger!

Looper Threaders can be as simple as a dental floss threader or as sophisticated as a threader that can be purchased as an added accessory.

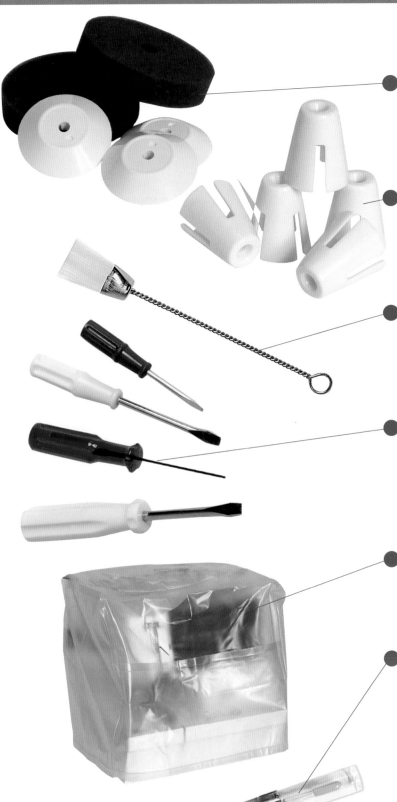

Spool Caps and Sponge Disks help anchor the cones so thread feeds off the spool pins much easier. These are a must when you use conventional parallel wound spools of thread.

Cone Holders hold the cones of thread firmly on the spool pins. Sometimes, the holders get caught in the cones and you'll wonder where you hid them the next time you change thread colors.

Lint Brushes are used to remove the lint that accumulates during serging. They are very important tools, as a clean serger has fewer stitching problems!

Screwdrivers come in handy for changing needles, blades, presser feet, needle plates and any other parts that need to be removed for cleaning, oiling or replacing. One or two sizes of screwdrivers are usually included with your serger.

Vinyl Dust Covers are great for keeping dust off your serger when not in use. If you live in a very humid climate, a fabric cover might be a better choice.

Oilers keep your serger lubricated and humming along. Check your manual to see how often and where you should oil your serger. Clean your serger before oiling! A fine-point oiler allows you to get into the smaller parts of the machine and prevents "over-oiling." Be sure to use oil that is meant to be used on your serger (check your manual) and *never* use household oil, which is too heavy for your machine.

Optional Supplies

Many optional supplies are available at your local sewing and notion retailers. Here are some that are very helpful. Read the brief descriptions, take a look at the pictures and then judge for yourself.

Fabric Swatches for testing stitches can be used to test thread compatibility, tension, stitch length and stitch width. Cut small pieces of fabric in various weights to simulate items you plan to sew or use scraps from existing projects. (Have pieces of knit, cotton, Lycra® and denim in your swatch pack.)

4" x 6" Serger Reference Cards track your serger project information so you can replicate your last serged masterpiece!

Surgical Seam Rippers quickly cut unwanted threads. You should have a surgeon's license to use this sharp tool!

Two-Needle Installer® holds one or two needles for installation and tightening at once. Quick and easy!

Bob 'n Serge houses filled bobbins for serging. Be frugal and wind several bobbins from one cone of thread and place them in this handy gadget. (One set of filled bobbins will serge an adult T-shirt.)

Double Eyed Needles are used to nab the thread tail and weave it back through the stitches to secure an end.

Serger Pads/Trim Catchers help keep all the serger snippets at bay! Use a serger pad and you won't have to chase your serger all over your sewing table.

SergerTilt™ is definitely an ergonomically friendly solution for safer serging, especially if you have back problems. The SergerTilt™ raises the back of the machine for better visibility and stitching ease.

Canned Air helps remove dust from your serger. Make sure you use a product that is environmentally friendly and don't dust your whole sewing room with it—even if it needs it!

Mini Vacuum Attachments help keep your serger clean! Not a necessity, but a great gift.

Seam Sealants seal all those edges on napkins or other projects that you want finished with a quick-fuse method. Don't be without this!

Booklets and Workbooks are more "in-depth" help than the manual that comes with your machine. They usually include easy projects for practicing techniques and a place to put samples you have made. Samples are a great reference tool.

Serger Cases and Trolleys are soft-sided, padded compartments that protect your machine when carrying it to class. Most feature wheels and retractable handles which make it much easier to maneuver.

Flower Head Pins are extra long (2"), so you need fewer pins for each seam.

Note from Nancy

I like to use Flower Head Pins when serging. I place the pins parallel to the seam to avoid contact with the blade. The flower heads lie flat against the fabric, yet they're easy to grasp when you're serging a seam.

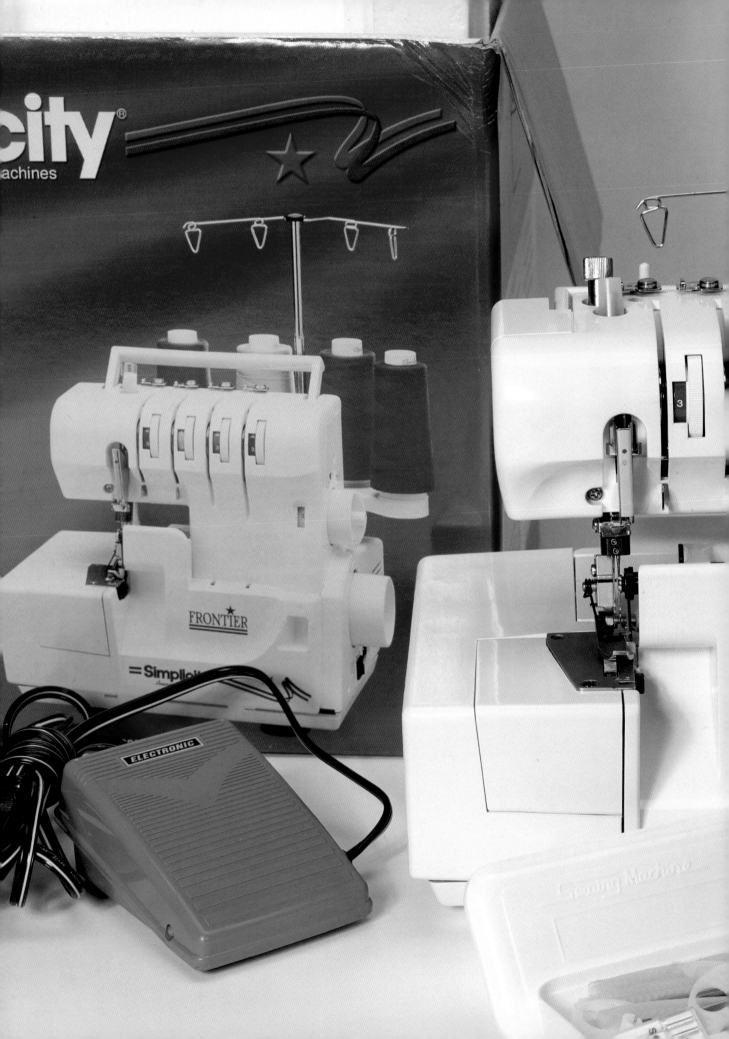

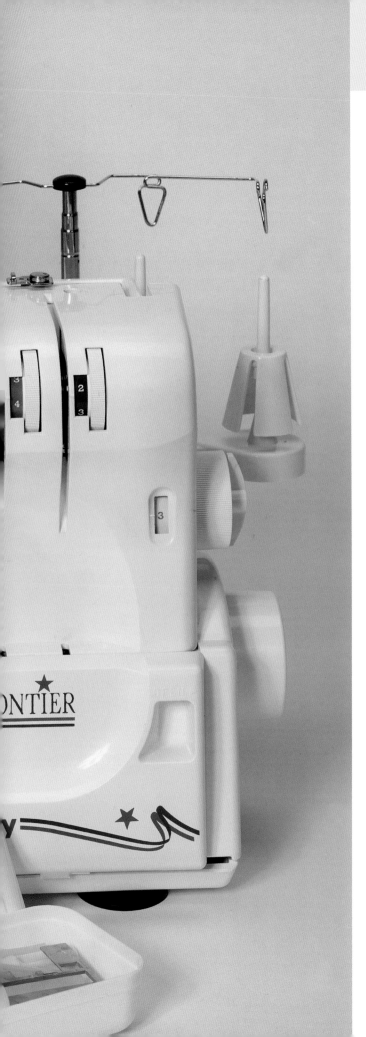

chapter 2

Get Set to Serge— Almost There . . .

Taking the machine "out of the box" is the most difficult step in serging. The salesperson made everything look so easy, but now you need to muster the confidence to set it up and stitch those first simple seams. Take the journey with me; I will help you every step of the way.

Setting Up Your Serger

Take the machine out of the box. I know all those dials and antenna look kind of intimidating. You can do it! It's time to bond with your serger!

- Remove the instruction manual and the accessories.

- Record your serial number on your purchase information and put it, along with your receipt, in a file for safekeeping.

- Position the serger on a serger pad, unless your serger has strong suction cups to hold it in place. The pad minimizes vibration and machine movement.

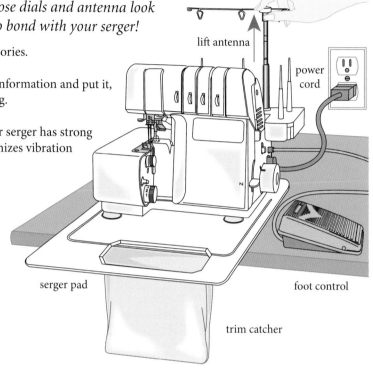

Note from Nancy

Attach a trim catcher. Some sergers are blessed with them; they come attached! The trim catcher protects you and your sewing area from the messy lint that is left as seams are trimmed. Some trim catchers also double as a serger pad to keep your machine from hopping around when serging at high speeds.

- Use a soft, clean cloth or 100% cotton balls to gently wipe any machine parts that may touch your fabric. The machine was oiled at the factory and oil often accumulates when it sits without use.

- Attach your spool base and antenna, if not already attached, following instructions in your manual.

- Attach the cone holders or sponge disks and spool caps, depending on the type of thread you are planning to use.

- Lift the antenna (thread guide pole) to the highest position. This prevents uneven stitches and keeps the thread from tangling.

- Plug the foot control into the machine base. (The socket is usually located on the lower right side of the machine.) Plug the machine power cord into your electrical outlet.

- Go back over the various parts of the serger to familiarize yourself with your new friend!

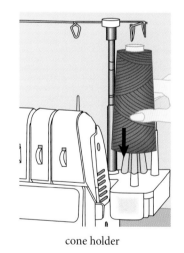

cone holder

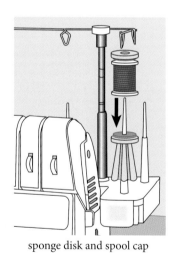

sponge disk and spool cap

Note from Nancy

Put all the styrofoam and plastic that you will not be using back in the box. Save the box "just in case" you ever need to transport the machine; for example, when you are moving or if you need to send the machine to the manufacturer.

Threading Your 4-Thread Serger

There are basically three methods for threading a serger: Fresh Start, Tie-On and Jet-Air Threading™. Threading most sergers is done in a specific thread order. The upper looper is first, then the lower looper and finally the needles. Check your instruction manual to confirm the proper sequence for your serger.

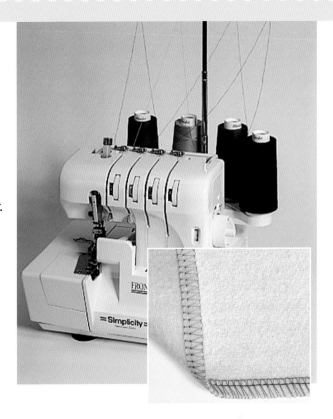

Note from **Nancy**

If this is the very first time you have threaded your machine, you might want to thread each looper and needle with a different color thread. Coordinate with your threading chart. After you complete your threading, you will be able to see at a glance how each thread functions and where it ends up in the serged stitching. Besides, it's much more colorful!

Fresh-Start Threading

Just as the name implies, this is threading from the very beginning. Even if your machine comes already threaded, it is a good idea to rethread so you learn how it is done. Sometimes, the threads get tangled in shipping, so if you try to "tie-on" and stitch, you end up with a mess!

Upper Looper

- Make sure your thread antenna is in its highest position.

- Thread the upper looper as recommended in your instruction manual. Thread each of the guides for that looper. Make sure the loopers aren't crossed. Turn the hand wheel a small amount to get the right position. Thread the eye of the upper looper. Then go back and double-check that you haven't missed any guides.

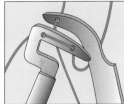

correct looper threading   incorrect: crossed loopers

Lower Looper

- Thread the lower looper, making sure you thread each of the guides for that looper. Go back and double-check them.

- Use a looper threader and/or tweezers to help you thread the lower looper.

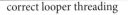

Needles

- Thread the needles **after** looper threading has been completed. The right needle is usually threaded first, followed by the left needle. It is important that the needles are threaded last so the needle thread doesn't run under the looper threads. If the looper threads break, you also will need to rethread the needles. (Not necessary on sergers with Jet-Air Threading™ and tubular loopers. Because there is no exposed thread and no thread guides, the serger can be threaded in any order.)
  - Follow the thread guides for each of the needles, making sure the thread is engaged in the tension discs.
  - Verify that the thread has been placed through all of the thread guides. Then thread the needles.

Tie-On Threading

Once you have your serger threaded for the first time, you can tie-on to thread it in the future. (This procedure is not recommended for Jet-Air Threading™ machines.)

1 Clip all of the threads close to the thread cones.

2 Tie the new threads onto the original threads with an overhand knot.

3 Jot down initial tension settings so you can easily duplicate them when threading is finished. Then loosen tensions on all threads by turning the dials to the lowest numbers.

4 With the presser foot still in the raised position, carefully pull each of the looper threads separately through the machine. Trim excess thread as the new color is retrieved in the back of the presser foot.

5 Clip needle threads just above the eye of the needle. Raise the presser foot and pull the threads until the new threads near the eye. Clip the knots and insert a new thread through the eye of each needle.

6 Return tension dials to original settings. Test stitching on a fabric scrap.

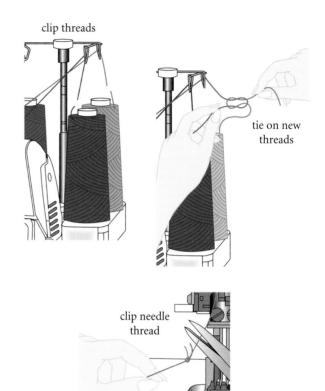

clip threads

tie on new threads

clip needle thread

Jet-Air Threading™

With the unique Jet-Air Threading™ system, available on many Baby Lock® models, a whoosh of air completes the looper threading process.

1 Close the tubular loopers by pressing the button near the thread ports, while turning the hand wheel toward you. You will hear the loopers close with a click.

2 Place thread through the antenna and tension guides designated for a looper.

3 Position thread in the correct port and press the looper threader lever.

4 Thread the needles the same as for other sergers. Use the built-in needle threader to complete threading.

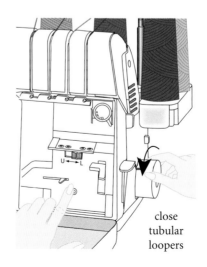

close tubular loopers

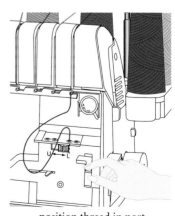

position thread in port

Jet-Air Thread Cradle for Decorative Threads

A thread cradle works well for getting heavier or decorative threads through the Jet-Air thread port.

1 Cut 1 yard of thread; fold it in half.

2 Clip thread ends even; insert them into the thread port.

3 Depress the thread mechanism while holding onto the thread. Thread ends will be drawn through the machine, leaving a thread loop resembling a lasso.

4 Insert the decorative thread through the lasso. Pull the thread ends of the cradle through the looper, bringing the decorative thread along with it.

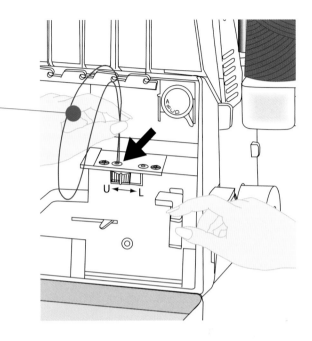

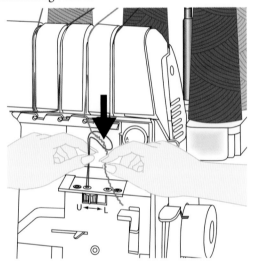

Note from **Nancy**

If you forget to hang on to the folded end of the thread cradle, it will shoot across the room as it is forced through the thread port!

Test Serging

Now you're ready to serge! Test your stitches on scrap fabric similar to the fabric you're using for your project.

1 Lower the presser foot and take a few stitches by turning the hand wheel. Make sure that stitches are forming on the stitch finger. If they are, slowly press the foot pedal and serge a chain about 3" long. Bring chain under the back of the presser foot.

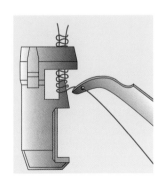

2 Fold your scrap fabric in half and begin to serge. The stitches should form on the fabric and the movable blade should trim off any excess to the right of the needles.

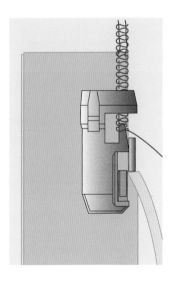

Serger Adjustments

You may need to fine-tune serger settings to obtain different types of stitches and to make sure your stitches are balanced on various fabrics. Most machines have provisions for adjusting tension, stitch width and length, the blade, differential feed and pressure. Check your instruction manual for specifics.

Tension

Tension mechanisms control the interlocking point of your serger threads. Adjusting tension is an essential serging skill. It is important to know what a balanced stitch looks like and which tension dial controls each thread. Check your instruction manual for specifics. Additional information on achieving a balanced stitch can be found in the "Troubleshooting" section, pages 119 through 125. Some sergers control tension automatically, while others have knobs or dials for adjusting tension.

- **Automatically controlled tension:** If your serger automatically adjusts the tension, there isn't a visible tension control. The proper amount of thread is measured and released automatically to adjust the tension. It is still important to understand basic thread tensions so you know when there is a problem with your machine or the thread you are using.

balanced tension   unbalanced tension

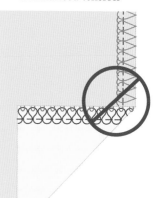

A Well-Balanced 4-Thread Stitch:

- *Needle threads are taut on each side.*

- *The upper looper thread rides on the edge of the fabric.*

- *The lower looper thread is not visible on the right side of the fabric.*

- **Tension inset dials:** Inset dials focus on numbers; the larger the number, the more tension on the thread and the tighter the stitch.

- **Tension knobs:** Outer knobs are used to control the tension. On some sergers, they make one complete rotation, while others (especially older models) have no numbers and make several rotations.
  - Turn the knob clockwise to tighten tension.
  - Turn the knob counterclockwise to loosen tension.

Stitch Width

Stitch width adjusts the height of the overlock stitch by moving the blade closer to or farther away from the needles. A larger number will produce a wider stitch and a smaller number will make a narrower stitch. The stitch width is measured from the needle hole to the cut edge of the fabric.

Wide Stitch Widths
- Used on heavier fabrics and with heavier decorative threads.

- Loosen looper tensions if necessary.

Narrow Stitch Widths
- Used for finishing lightweight fabrics and in decorative applications such as pintucks, rolled edges and flatlocking fine ribbons and laces.

- Tighten looper or needle tensions if necessary.

Refer to your instruction manual for specific directions on setting the stitch width for your serger.

Stitch Length

Stitch length determines how close individual stitches are to each other. The smaller the number, the closer together the stitches are and the larger the number, the farther apart the stitches are. The length can usually be adjusted from less than 1 mm to about 5 mm, but may vary from one serger to the next. Some experts refer to the stitch length as the distance between the needle holes from one stitch to the next.

Smaller number (stitches are closer together):
- Set when you are edge finishing or stitching on a lighter-weight fabric.

- Tighten looper tensions if necessary.

Larger number (stitches are farther apart):
- Set when using heavy decorative threads and stitching on heavier fabrics.

- Loosen looper tensions if necessary.

Refer to your instruction manual for specific directions on setting the stitch length for your serger.

Serger Blades

The terms "blades" and "knives" are used synonymously by different companies when referring to the same part of the serger. For all practical purposes, we will use the term blades.

Sergers distinctively have two blades that work together to trim the fabric as you serge.

- A moving blade
- A stationary blade

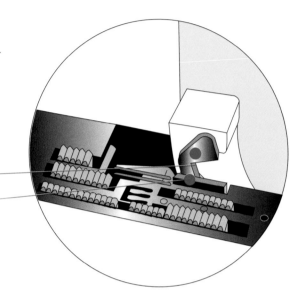

Disengaging the Moving Blade

Disengaging the moving blade allows you to stitch close to the blade position without having to worry about your project being trimmed—especially if it is a folded edge. The process for disengaging the moving blade varies. Check your instruction manual for instructions specific to your serger. Disengage the moving blade primarily for decorative stitching (such as flatlocking), chain stitching and cover stitching.

Options for disengaging moving blade:

- Turn up and out of the way.
- Turn down.
- Lock in down position.

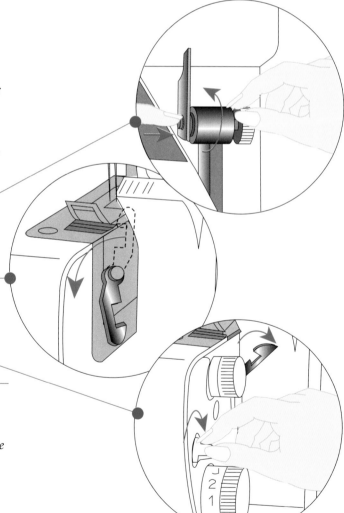

Note from Nancy

If too much fabric extends past the knife when it is disengaged, the fabric will most likely get caught in the upper looper. That can spell disaster for your project!

Differential Feed

Feed dogs are the jagged metal teeth in the bed of the serger, under the presser foot, that feed the fabric through the machine. A serger has two sets of feed dogs: one in front and one in back. The two feed dogs generally feed at the same rate during serging. However, on some machines, the two feed dogs are able to move independently; the front feed dog can move faster or slower than the back feed dog. This ability is termed "differential feed."

- Differential feed set to a larger number will ease or gather fabric.

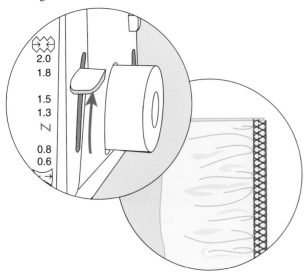

- Differential feed set to a smaller number will build stretch into a seam.

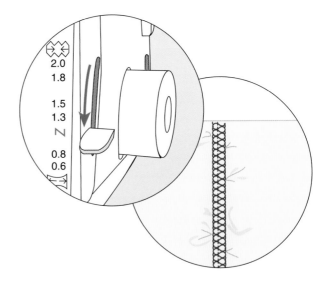

Note from **Nancy**

If you have a difficult time remembering which way to change the differential feed, remember this little saying: "More to ease; less to stretch!"

Pressure Bolt or Screw

To adjust the pressure bolt or screw, usually located on top of the serger, remember the mechanic's rule: "Righty tighty, lefty loosey!" This adjustment is especially helpful if your machine does not have differential feed.

- Turn the bolt to the right (clockwise) to increase pressure. This keeps the fabric from slipping, for example, when serging on lightweight or silky fabric.

- Turn the bolt to the left (counterclockwise) to decrease pressure. This avoids stretching knits and skipping stitching on heavy fabrics or knits.

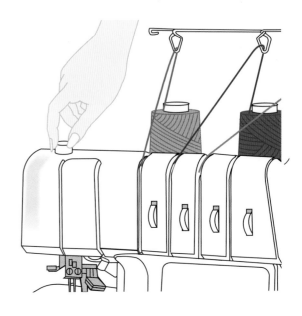

Stitch Types and Setup

4-Thread Overlock Stitch

The 4-thread overlock is the most basic stitch on a serger. It is strong and reinforced—a perfect stitch on denim—yet it can be used on stretch fabrics because it has a fair amount of "give." This stitch uses two needles plus the upper and lower loopers; hence, the name 4-thread overlock. On most sergers, the left needle in a 4-thread stitch is ¼" from the cutting blade.

Note from Nancy

Sergers in the ready-to-wear industry use a ¼" seam and the process of serging with a ¼" seam was originally called "marrowing." This is why the "M" is used on the stitch width dial of many sergers. It doesn't stand for "middle" as most people think … rather "marrow" width setting for ¼" seams.

4-Thread Overlock

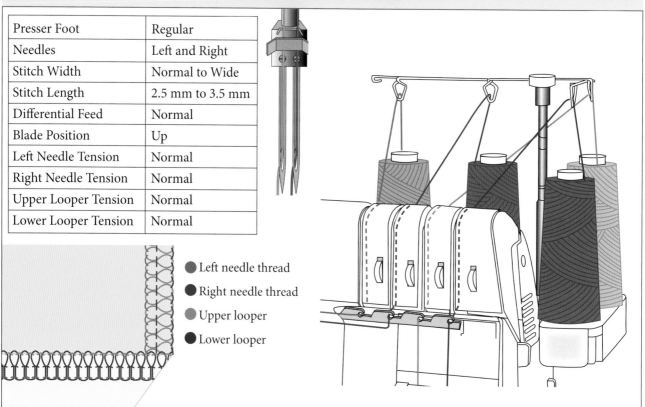

Presser Foot	Regular
Needles	Left and Right
Stitch Width	Normal to Wide
Stitch Length	2.5 mm to 3.5 mm
Differential Feed	Normal
Blade Position	Up
Left Needle Tension	Normal
Right Needle Tension	Normal
Upper Looper Tension	Normal
Lower Looper Tension	Normal

- ● Left needle thread
- ● Right needle thread
- ● Upper looper
- ● Lower looper

Check your instruction manual for any settings unique to your serger. For example, some machines have a Stitch Selector dial.

Serging a 4-Thread Overlock

1 Chain off 2" to 3".

2 Start to feed fabric under the presser foot. It is not necessary to completely lift the presser foot. Many sergers have a spring foot. Slightly lift the front of the foot to get the fabric to feed.

3 Position the fabric.
   • With ⅝" seam allowances, use the ⅝" seam guide. The seam will be trimmed to ¼" as you serge.

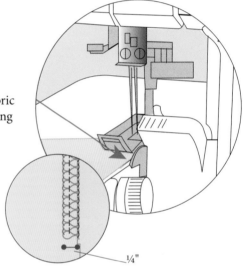

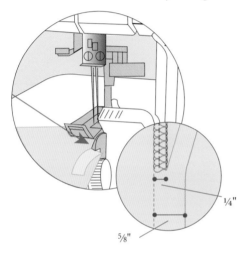

   • With ¼" seam allowances, guide fabric to the left of the cutting blade.

4-Thread Overlock Applications

Seaming Wovens

Fabrics that tend to ravel, especially when used in children's clothing, need this security stitch. Loosen looper tensions to prevent fabric from bunching if necessary. On heavier wovens, such as denim, set the stitch width to a wider setting and loosen looper tensions.

Seaming Knits

Use 4-thread knit seams in high-stress areas, especially in knit sportswear. These fabrics need to have secure seams and yet have enough stretch to "give" with the activity.

When you serge shoulder seams on a stretchy knit, you may want to stabilize the seams using twill tape or ribbon. Feed the ribbon or twill tape under the presser foot and on top of the seam. Some sergers have a special slot in front of the presser foot to accommodate various stabilizer tapes.

Seaming Patchwork

The ¼" marrowed seam is a quilter's delight! Use when strip quilting. Serge strips and subcut into sections.

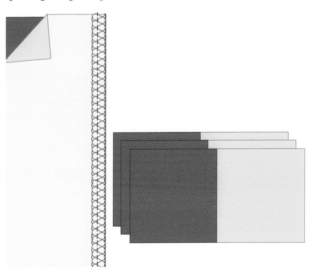

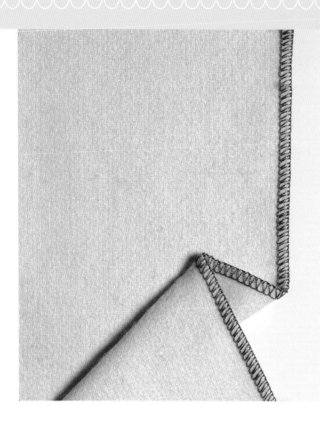

3-Thread Overlock Stitch— Narrow

A 3-thread overlock stitch has more stretch built into it than the 4-thread overlock and also conserves thread. Use it on seams that don't require the extra stability of the second needle thread. You will have one needle thread and two looper threads (upper and lower) overcasting the edges. To obtain a narrow 3-thread, use the right needle. For a wide 3-thread stitch, use the left needle.

Note from **Nancy**

Whenever you remove or replace a needle, remember to securely tighten the needle clamp screw. Otherwise, the screw may loosen and come flying off due to the vibration created as you serge.

3-Thread Overlock—Narrow

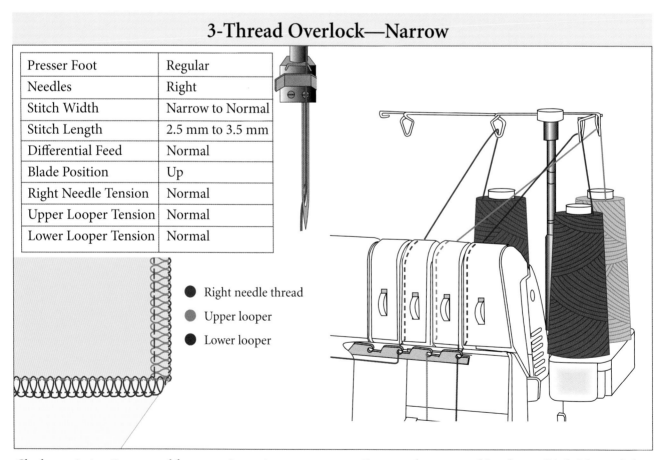

Presser Foot	Regular
Needles	Right
Stitch Width	Narrow to Normal
Stitch Length	2.5 mm to 3.5 mm
Differential Feed	Normal
Blade Position	Up
Right Needle Tension	Normal
Upper Looper Tension	Normal
Lower Looper Tension	Normal

- Right needle thread
- Upper looper
- Lower looper

Check your instruction manual for any settings unique to your serger. For example, some machines have a Stitch Selector dial.

Narrow 3-Thread Overlock Applications

Seaming Knits

The 3-thread overlock provides durability and stretch for seaming light- to medium-weight stretchy knits such as lingerie, swimwear and interlock. Use Woolly Nylon thread in needle and loopers for extra stretch and softness.

Lycra

Adjust differential feed to a smaller number to build stretch into the seam.

Lingerie

Set the differential feed to a larger number to prevent distorting the knit. This adjustment is usually necessary if loops hang off the edge of the serged fabric. You may need to adjust stitch width or looper tensions.

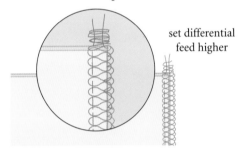

set differential feed higher

Overcasting Seams

Overcasting seams with a 3-thread overlock keeps them from raveling, gives a neat finished look to the project and doesn't add bulk.

Seams Pressed to One Side

- Serge seams, guiding the fabric along the ⅝" marking on your serger. The seam will be trimmed to ¼". If the pattern includes a ¼" seam allowance, guide the fabric to the left of the cutting blade so it will not be trimmed.
- Press seams flat to set the stitches and then press them to one side.

Seams Pressed Open

- Serge all seam edges before construction without cutting off any fabric. If you serge notched areas, remember to mark them with a fabric marker.

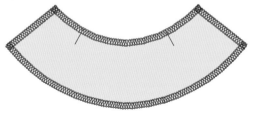

- Stitch ⅝" seams with a conventional sewing machine.
- Press seams flat to set the stitches, then press them open.

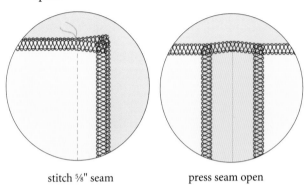

stitch ⅝" seam   press seam open

Serging a Narrow Hem

A 3-thread overlock makes an eye-catching narrow hem, great for facings, table linens, ruffles and hemlines on lightweight woven fabrics.

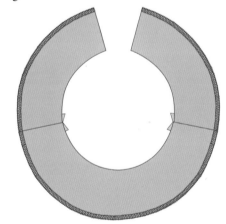

Note from Nancy

The narrow 3-thread overlock is awesome for serging fun things like "Serger Twists" and "Serger Diamond Tucks," as on pages 63 and 64.

Ribbing Application

Although the methods of applying ribbing discussed in this section are intended for neckline ribbing, you'll find the techniques can be adapted for use on cuffs and bottom bands.

Flat Method for Neckline Ribbing
This is the easiest method of applying ribbing with a serger!

1   Serge one shoulder seam, right sides together.

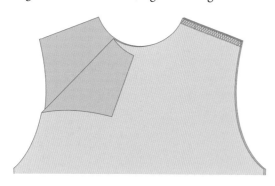

Note from Nancy

I like to include a piece of Stay-Tape or ribbon in the seam as I serge to stabilize the shoulder seam.

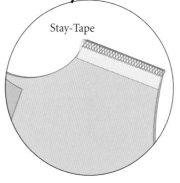

Stay-Tape

---

2   Attach the neckline ribbing.
   • Fold ribbing in half lengthwise, wrong sides together.

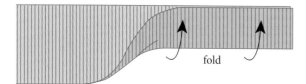

fold

   • Quarter the ribbing and neckline, using the center front and center back as two of the points. Mark quarter points with pins or a marking pen. Remember that the shoulder seams are not equidistant from the center front and back— measure!

   • Pin the shirt and ribbing right sides together, matching quarter marks.

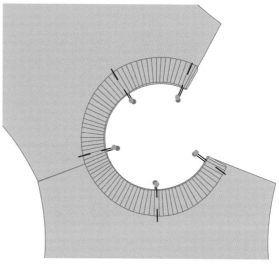

   • Stretch the ribbing to meet the neckline.
   • Serge the ribbing to the neckline with the ribbing on the top. Be careful to match cut edges of ribbing to unsewn shoulder seam. Don't forget to remove pins as you get to them!

3   Serge the remaining ribbing and shoulder seam, right sides together, stabilizing the shoulder seam if desired. The ribbing ends should match at the neckline edge.

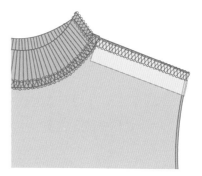

Circular Method for Neckline Ribbing

This method of applying ribbing is the neatest finish, but it is a bit more challenging.

1 Serge both shoulder seams, right sides together. Stabilize the seams, if desired. (See Note, page 32.)

2 Meet the short ends of the ribbing, right sides together. Sew a conventional seam using a sewing machine, as it is much less bulky. Finger press seam open.

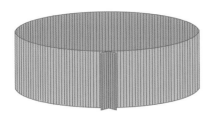

3 Fold the ribbing in half lengthwise, wrong sides together, meeting cut edges.

4 Quarter the ribbing and the neckline, using center back and center front as two of the matching points.

5 Position ribbing seam at the center back of the neckline. It will not only look better, but you will always be able to tell the shirt front from the back.

6 Serge with ribbing on the right side of the fabric, stretching the fabric from one quarter point to the next.

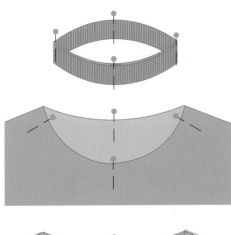

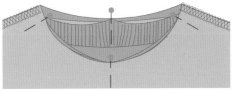

7 When you approach the starting point, take a few stitches over previous stitching. Then taper the stitching off the fabric, leaving a 2" to 3" thread tail.

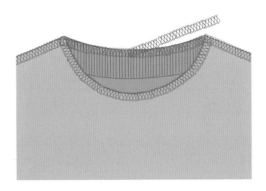

8 Thread one of the eyes on a double eyed needle with the thread tail and work it back through the seam. (See page 57.) Optional: Add a drop of seam sealant. A small amount is sufficient. A larger amount may be scratchy on the neckline.

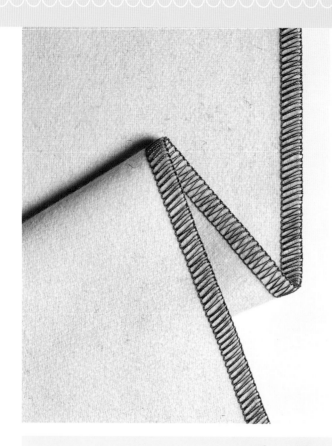

3-Thread Overlock Stitch— Wide

The wide 3-thread overlock is typically used for decorative trim, but it can also be used to seam heavy knits and overcast medium to heavy, easily fraying fabrics. Use decorative specialty threads in the upper looper or use it in both the upper and lower loopers for reversible borders.

3-Thread Overlock—Wide

Presser Foot	Regular
Needles	Left
Stitch Width	Wide
Stitch Length	1 mm to 4 mm
Differential Feed	Normal
Blade Position	Up
Left Needle Tension	Normal
Upper Looper Tension	Normal
Lower Looper Tension	Normal

● Left needle thread
● Upper looper
● Lower looper

Check your instruction manual for any settings unique to your serger. For example, some machines have a Stitch Selector dial.

3-Thread Wide Applications

Seaming Heavyweight Knits

1 Use regular cone thread in both loopers and needle.

2 Test stitches with the length set at normal. Adjust as necessary for a nice looking seam.

Adding Decorative Edging

1 Use decorative threads in the loopers and regular cone thread in the needle.

2 Test stitches with the length set at normal. Adjust as necessary to accommodate the decorative threads.

3 Loosen upper and/or lower tensions.

4 Tighten lower looper tension if you are using a specialty thread in only the upper looper.

3-Thread Wave Stitch

The wave stitch is a decorative "wavy" stitch exclusive to Baby Lock®. The upper and lower looper threads alternate in appearance on the top side of the fabric about every 25 stitches, producing a wavy looking decorative stitch.

Basically, the wave is a 3-thread stitch in which the upper looper thread has been pulled with a rhythm to create the wave. It can be accomplished manually with a wide 3-thread stitch, but it is difficult to achieve a consistent wave pattern. The Baby Lock® Wave Serger has a built-in mechanism that automatically and precisely creates the wave stitch.

Use different-colored decorative threads in the upper and lower loopers for a spectacular finish!

3-Thread Wave

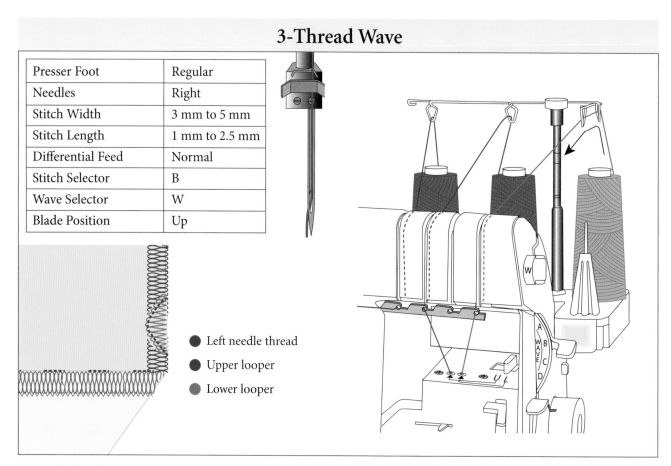

Presser Foot	Regular
Needles	Right
Stitch Width	3 mm to 5 mm
Stitch Length	1 mm to 2.5 mm
Differential Feed	Normal
Stitch Selector	B
Wave Selector	W
Blade Position	Up

● Left needle thread
● Upper looper
● Lower looper

Note: The threading pattern is unique for the wave stitch. Please check your instruction manual for specifics.

3-Thread Rolled Wave

The rolled wave stitch is a variation of the wave stitch and is used to finish napkins, tablecloths and other fine fabrics where a narrower wave is desired.

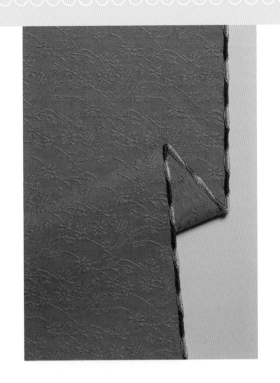

Note from Nancy

To produce a uniform stitch when serging the wave stitch, serge at a consistent speed, especially when using decorative threads in the loopers.

3-Thread Rolled Wave

Presser Foot	Regular
Needles	Right
Stitch Width	3 mm to 5 mm
Stitch Length	1 mm to 1.5 mm Rolled
Differential Feed	Normal
Stitch Selector	C
Wave Selector	W
Blade Position	Up

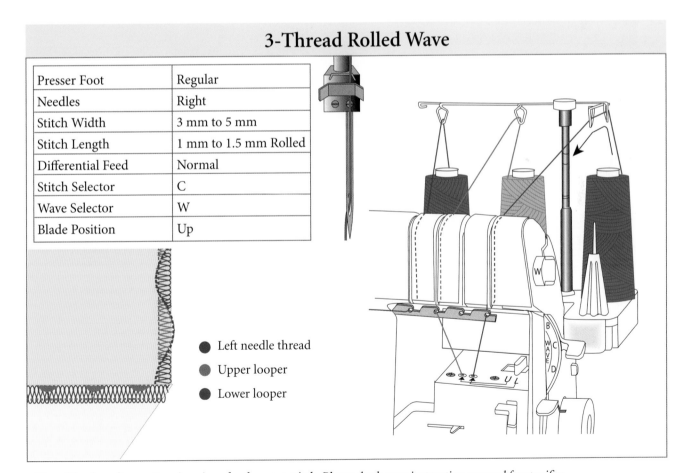

- ● Left needle thread
- ● Upper looper
- ● Lower looper

Note: The threading pattern is unique for the wave stitch. Please check your instruction manual for specifics.

3-Thread Rolled Edge

The rolled edge settings produce the narrowest serger stitch possible. Lower looper tension is tightened almost completely. Upper looper thread wraps around the edge of the fabric and the lower looper forms almost a straight line of stitching on the back of the fabric. On some sergers, the presser foot is changed to one with a narrower stitch finger. Some sergers require that you also use a special throat plate for rolled hemming. Check your instruction manual for your serger specifics.

3-Thread Rolled Edge

Presser Foot	Rolled Edge
Needles	Right
Stitch Width	Narrow to Normal
Stitch Length	1 mm to 2 mm (R)*
Differential Feed	Normal
Blade Position	Up
Right Needle Tension	Loosen
Lower Looper Tension	Tighten

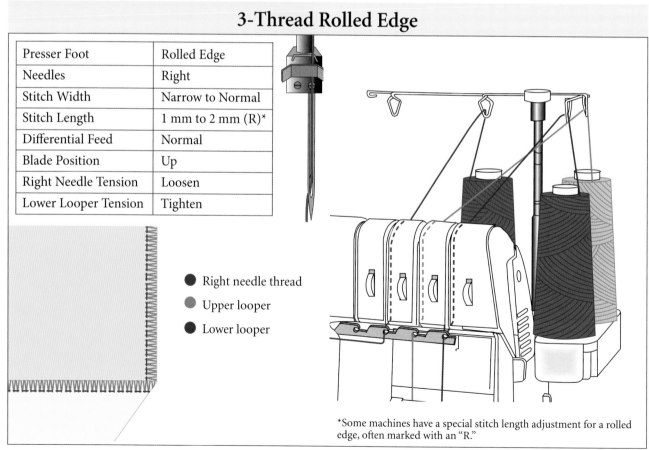

● Right needle thread
● Upper looper
● Lower looper

*Some machines have a special stitch length adjustment for a rolled edge, often marked with an "R."

3-Thread Rolled Edge Applications

A rolled edge is primarily used for hemming lightweight fabrics, but is also suitable for seaming sheer and lightweight fabrics. There are several decorative applications of this stitch, including pintucks, lettuce edges and piping. (See pages 66 and 67.)

Edge Finishing

Rolled edge hemming is especially nice on table linens and other lightweight fabrics.

Thread Options:

- Regular two-ply cone thread (needle, upper looper and lower looper)

- Rayon thread (needle, upper looper and lower looper)

- Woolly Nylon thread (upper looper and lower looper; regular serger cone thread in needle)

- Metallic (upper looper; regular serger cone thread in the needle and Woolly Nylon in the lower looper)

- Fine yarn such as Polyarn (texturized polyester) thread (upper looper; regular serger cone thread in needle and lower looper or use Woolly Nylon in the lower looper)

Note from Nancy

Use Woolly Nylon in the lower looper when you need a tighter tension for a rolled edge. This specialty thread contracts and pulls the upper looper thread around the edge. You will achieve tight, smooth rolled hems.

You can also use Woolly Nylon in the needle in addition to the loopers for soft knit edges. To make threading easier, put a drop of seam sealant such as FrayBlock™ or Fray Check™ on the tip of your finger and roll the needle thread end between your finger and thumb. Let dry and trim at an angle if necessary.

Seaming Sheer Fabrics

Rolled hems are excellent for sheer seams and for heirloom sewing applications such as entredeux, laces and fancy trims. Sheer seams would otherwise require time consuming French seams.

1 Adjust the serger for a basic rolled hem.

2 Thread the needle and both loopers with rayon or other decorative threads. Place thread nets over the spools to help thread feed freely and smoothly.

Note from Nancy

Place a thread net in the hole on the bottom of the thread spool, bring the net up over the thread and place the thread on the spindle. This method creates a small basket around the rayon thread so it doesn't pool at the bottom of the spool and get caught.

3 Test stitches on a fabric swatch on both the lengthwise and crosswise grains. Adjust tensions, length and width if necessary.

4 Stabilize the edge with a water-soluble stabilizer, such as Avalon® or Perfect Sew™. The stabilizer prevents the edge from stretching as you sew and prevents "pokies" (troublesome fibers that protrude at the edge).

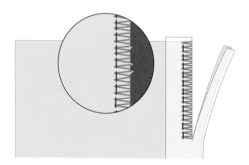

5 Remove the stabilizer with a spritz of water or by hand washing the project after serging is completed.

Note from Nancy

If you adjust your stitch length to about 2 mm and set your tensions back to normal, you can achieve a small unrolled serged edge. Use this stitch in areas such as shoulder seams on lightweight fabrics. You may want to add a reinforcing tape or a narrow selvage edge strip for stability.

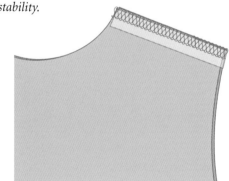

2-Thread Rolled Edge

Use right needle and lower looper for a 2-thread rolled edge stitch. Check your instruction manual to see if your machine has this capability. If so, it is the preferred method for hemming very soft fabrics.

1 Tighten needle thread to wrap the looper thread around the fabric edge.

2 If the fabric edge is not sufficiently rolled, tighten the needle thread more or decrease looper tension.

3 Engage the 2-Thread Converter. This is a spring type mechanism that fits in a small hole at the top of the upper looper. It "tricks" the upper looper into thinking it is threaded. The 2-Thread Converter can also be referred to as a Subsidiary Looper or Auxiliary Looper. We will be using the term 2-Thread Converter for all practical purposes.

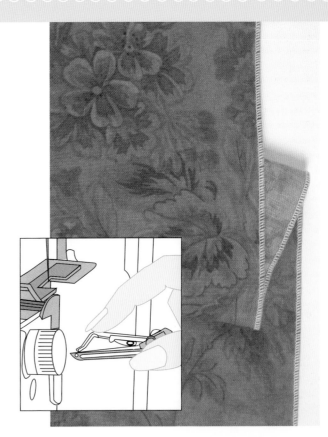

2-Thread Rolled Edge

Presser Foot	Rolled Edge
Needles	Left or Right
Stitch Width	Normal to Wider
Stitch Length	1 mm Left/0.5 mm Right
Differential Feed	Normal
Blade Position	Up
Right Needle Tension	Tighten
Lower Looper Tension	Normal or Loosen
2-Thread Converter	Engaged

● Right needle thread
● Lower looper

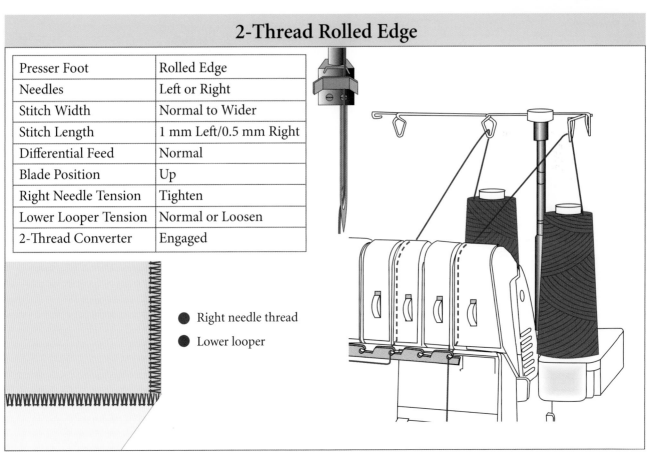

3-Thread Flatlock Stitch

Flatlock is an overlock method that forms a seam that when pulled, lies flat on the surface of the fabric. This stitch can be functional or used as a decorative accent on numerous garments or crafts. Embellishing creative projects is its forte; however, it is a very stretchy, durable seam to use on activewear and lingerie.

- Use the right needle for a narrow flatlock and the left needle for a wide flatlock.

- Choose coordinating or contrasting decorative threads for an elegant look. Don't underestimate the ease and versatility of this serging option.

Note from Nancy

*The key to a perfect flatlock is eliminating the needle tension. To do this, I remove the thread from the tension disc; then tighten the needle tension completely. The thread will ride over the disc with virtually **no tension** on the needle thread.*

3-Thread Flatlock–Wide or Narrow

Presser Foot	Regular
Needles	Left or Right
Stitch Width	Wide L/Normal R
Stitch Length	1 mm to 3 mm
Differential Feed	Normal
Blade Position	Down
L or R Needle Tension	Loosen
Upper Looper Tension	Tighten
Lower Looper Tension	Tighten

wide flatlock

narrow flatlock

- ● Right needle thread
- ● Upper looper
- ● Lower looper

Serging a 3-Thread Flatlock

Flatlocking is easy once you understand the basic principle. Serge a seam or the fold of a fabric; pull the two layers apart until the serging lies flat.

To determine which threads are visible in the finished project:

- Serge with wrong sides together to have looper thread(s) visible.

- Serge with right sides together to have the needle threads visible ("ladder stitches").

To flatlock a seam:

1 Position the cut edges about ⅛" away from the blade. Serge so the loops form slightly beyond the cut edges. Do not trim away any of the fabric.

2 Serge to the end of the seam, clearing the stitch finger. Then chain off the fabric for 3" to 4".

3 Pull the fabric layers apart until the stitches lie flat.

To flatlock within a project:

1 Fold the fabric at the desired position.

2 Place the folded edge approximately ⅛" away from the blade so the stitches form off the edge of the fabric. This makes it easy to flatten out the fabric after flatlocking is completed.

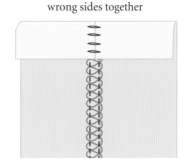
wrong sides together

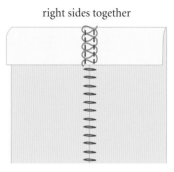
right sides together

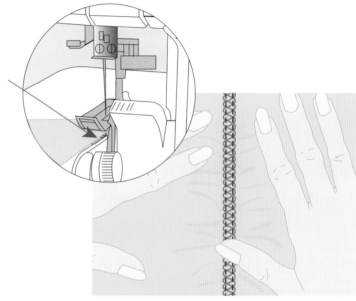
pull fabric apart until stitches lie flat

3-Thread Flatlock Applications

Decorative Trim (Ladder Stitch)

Embellish the ladder stitch by weaving ribbon and threads through it. For a special accent, add beads, knots, buttons and other trims to the ribbon or thread.

Note from **Nancy**

Using the ladder stitch is your chance to get creative with decorative threads in your lower looper, which would then show on the right side of your project.

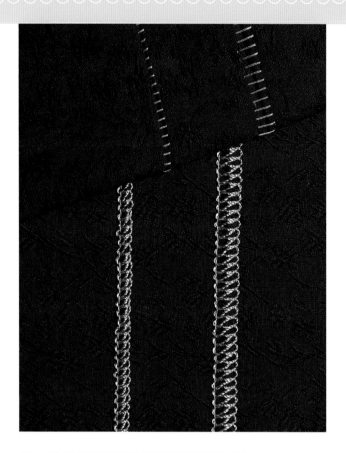

2-Thread Flatlock Stitch

The 2-thread flatlock stitch is not only more economical, but also less bulky for overedging fabrics such as wool. Flatlock seams are really a decorative application, as they show on the outside as well as the inside of the project. Specialty threads flatlocked on a garment or project add an artistic flair that's "uniquely you!"

Note from Nancy

Check your manual to make sure your serger is able to stitch with two threads; not all models have this feature. You need to have a 2-Thread Converter (a spring that closes the eye of the upper looper) to achieve this stitch.

2-Thread Flatlock Wide or Narrow

Presser Foot	Regular
Needles	Left or Right
Stitch Width	Wide L/Normal R
Stitch Length	2 mm to 3 mm
Differential Feed	Normal
Blade Position	Down
L or R Needle Tension	Loosen
2-Thread Converter	Engaged
Lower Looper Tension	Normal

wide flatlock

narrow flatlock

● Right needle t
● Lower looper

2-Thread Flatlock Applications

Decorative Seams and Topstitching

Fabrics that don't ravel (such as interlock knits, tricot, sweatshirt fleece and synthetic suede) are the best choice for 2-thread flatlock seams. If serged on a fold, the flatlock can create dramatic effects on the body of a garment or project. Either the ladder or loops can be used on the right side of the project. Use rayon thread or Woolly Nylon thread in the lower looper for an especially attractive look.

- Serge with wrong sides together and pull flat. The loops will be visible on the right side of the fabric.

- Serge with right sides together and pull flat. The ladder stitch will be visible on the right side of the fabric.

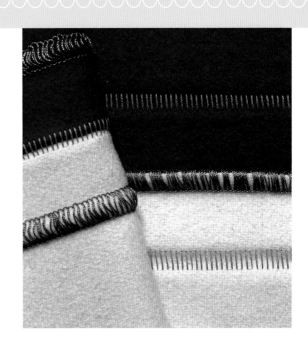

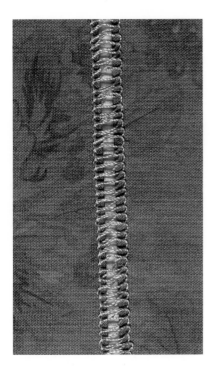

Serger Fagoting

Try something new like Serger Fagoting to revive your creative spirit! Create this decorative stitch by serging two folded edges together. Lace the stitches with ⅛" ribbon for a stunning effect.

1. Use a wide 2-thread flatlock (left needle).

2. Loosen needle tension to about -3 and tighten upper looper tension to about +1. Adjust as necessary.

3. Fold each fabric at the area where the flatlock will be, wrong sides together. Lay one of the fabrics on top of the other, right sides together, meeting folded edges.

4. Align the folds approximately ⅛" to ¼" from the cutting blade, so the flatlock loops hang halfway over the edge of the fabric.

5. Disengage the cutting blade.

6. Serge. Clear stitch fingers (see "Locked End," page 56) and chain off the fabric.

7. Gently pull fabric to flatten the stitches.

Overcasting

Use the narrow 2-thread flatlock to overcast edges without bulk. This is especially nice to use on wool.

Stitch with right side up and trim edges while overcasting for a clean finish.

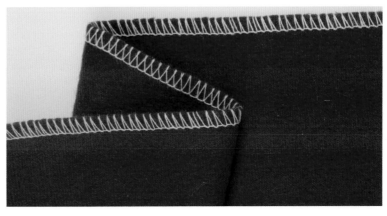

Cover Stitch (narrow, wide and triple)

*A cover stitch is both functional and decorative. Some sergers now feature up to 10 threads. These machines often can be converted to stitch a cover stitch. Other cover stitch sergers are stand-alone machines, which stitch **only** a cover stitch and a chain stitch. They do not have a blade mechanism and they cannot stitch an overlock, rolled edge or flatlock.*

Note from Nancy

You need to have a machine that is a combination overlock/ coverlock/chain stitch serger or a cover stitch/chain stitch serger to utilize these stitches. Check your instruction manual to see if your serger is capable of serging a cover stitch.

To prepare your serger for a cover stitch:

1   Thread and prepare the machine following instructions in the instruction manual. On machines capable of stitching an overlock, cover or disengage the serger blades and the upper looper.

2   Cut all needle threads to 4". Place threads to the left of the presser foot.

3   Place the fabric under the presser foot, directly below the needles.

4   Turn the hand wheel toward you to form two or three stitches.

5   Start to serge **slowly**. All basic overlock machines are able to stitch without fabric underneath the presser foot. However, when serging a cover stitch, it's advisable to start stitching directly on fabric and to use an anchor cloth (a small fabric remnant) at the end of the line of stitching. Again, check your instruction manual for recommendations.

6   Butt an anchor cloth to the line of cover stitching; chain off onto the anchor cloth. This prevents "stitch jams" under the presser foot. On some cover stitch machines, this is not necessary or it only needs to be done at initial set-up. Check your instruction manual.

7   Clip the threads between the anchor cloth and the project.

Note from Nancy

Always test the stitching on a scrap before serging on the project. It is much easier to make adjustments before working on your actual project. And there is a lot less "reverse serging!"

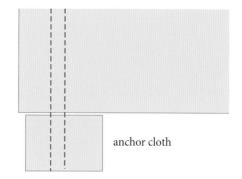

anchor cloth

Narrow Cover Stitch Applications

Use the center and right needles or the center and left needles with the chain looper to produce a narrow cover stitch. This stitch simulates a double-needle stitch on top of the fabric. The chain looper is visible on the underside of the fabric. If you would like the chain to be visible on the right side of the fabric, serge with the wrong side up. This creates a very decorative stitch when a specialty thread such as rayon is used in the chain looper.

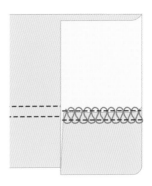

Hemming Fine Knits

1   Use regular serger cone thread matching the garment in needles and in the chain looper. Or, use a finer thread as desired.

2   Fold hem to the wrong side of the garment.

3   Stitch from the top side of the fabric with needles aligned to catch the top of the hem allowance. Fabric guides are available on some cover stitch machines to help position your fabric. This is especially helpful for stitching in the round, when altering ready-to-wear or when making a new garment.

Attaching Trim

Place trim on the right side of the fabric and topstitch it with the cover stitch. This is especially nice for ribbon and small braid trim.

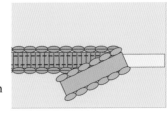

Note from Nancy

Wash-A-Way Wonder Tape works great to hold the trim in place on washable fabrics while you serge and it completely washes out later.

Narrow Left or Right Cover Stitch

Presser Foot	Regular
Needles	L or R plus Center
Stitch Width	Normal
Stitch Length	3 mm to 4 mm
Differential Feed	Normal
Blade Position	Down
L or R Needle Tension	4 to 6
Center Needle Tension	4 to 6
Chain Looper Tension	Cover or 1 mm to 3 mm
Add Stitch Table	
Disengage Upper Looper	

● Right needle thread

● Center needle thread

● Chain looper

Wide Cover Stitch

Use the left and right needles along with the chain looper to produce the widest cover stitch. This stitch is used widely in the ready-to-wear industry for hemming knit and woven garments. It is generally used with the double stitch on the right side, but in other instances the chain looper adds a charming accent to the right side of a garment.

Wide Cover Stitch Applications

Hemming Knits and Wovens

Use the same technique as for hemming with a narrow cover stitch. (See page 47.)

Shadow Work

1. Set up the serger with regular serger cone thread in the needles and a heavier thread such as 12 wt. cotton in the chain looper. The thread should contrast with the base fabric.

2. Use a transparent fabric, such as batiste or organdy, so the chain looper thread will be visible shadowing through the fabric.

3. Use a medium stitch width and a 3.0 stitch length.

4. Mark stitching lines on the sheer transparent fabric.

5. Cover stitch along marked lines.

6. Back the transparent fabric with a layer of cotton fabric to match the base fabric. This brings out the shadow work.

Wide Cover Stitch

Presser Foot	Regular
Needles	Left, Center, Right
Stitch Length	3 mm to 4 mm
Differential Feed	Normal
Blade Position	Down
L or R Needle Tension	4 to 6
Chain Looper Tension	Cover/Normal
Add Stitch Table	
Disengage Upper Looper	

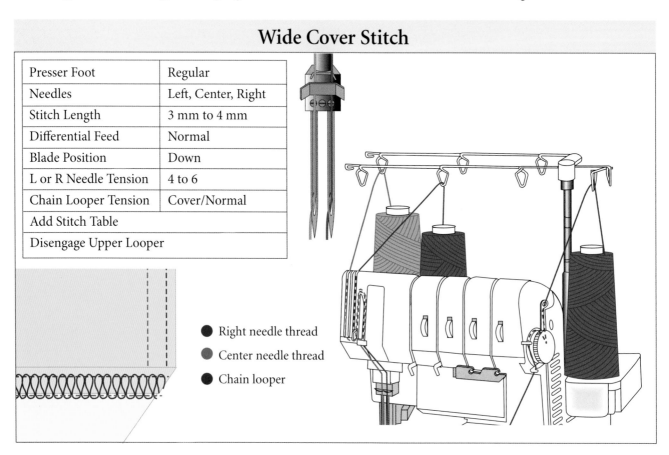

● Right needle thread

● Center needle thread

● Chain looper

Triple Cover Stitch

Using three needles produces three parallel rows of cover stitching. This stitching appears on the right side of the fabric, providing the fabric is right side up during serging. Use the triple cover stitch for decorative hems and attaching trim. It is excellent for stitching belt loops with a Belt Loop Binder attachment. (See page 79.)

Setup is basically the same as for the wide cover stitch, except that you add another needle to the center position of the needle holder. Tension on that needle is still within the 4 to 6 range.

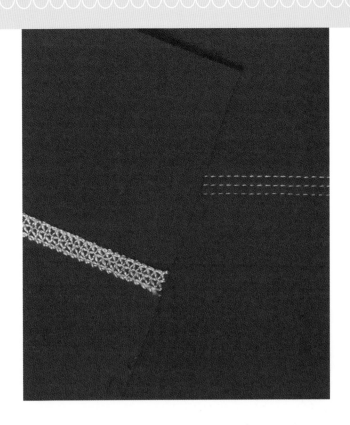

Triple Cover Stitch

Presser Foot	Regular
Needles	Left and Right
Stitch Length	3 mm to 4 mm
Differential Feed	Normal
Blade Position	Down
L or R Needle Tension	4 to 6
Chain Looper Tension	Cover/Normal
Add Stitch Table	
Disengage Upper Looper	

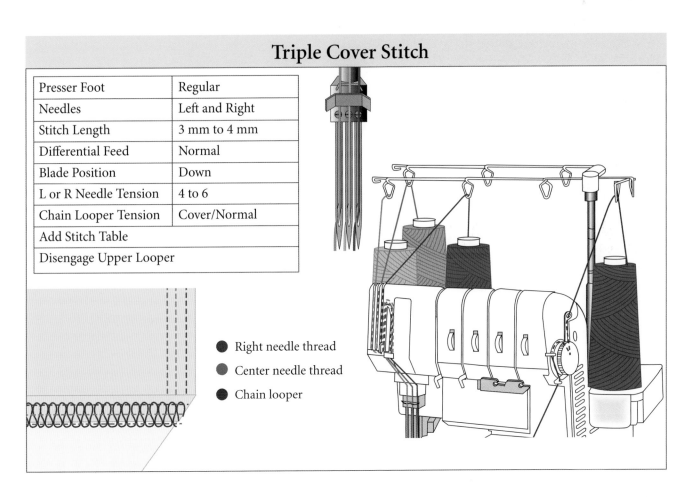

● Right needle thread

● Center needle thread

● Chain looper

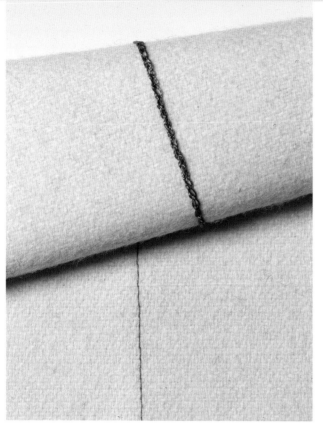

Chain Stitch

Eliminate all but one of the cover stitch needles and you'll have a chain stitch. Some sergers are set up so the left needle stitches a ⅝" seam allowance, the middle needle a ½" seam allowance and the right needle a ⅜" seam allowance.

Note from Nancy

You can find a chain stitch used in very functional ways—the closure on a bag of dog food or a bag of water softener salt! From the topside, it looks like a regular machine stitch, but the back of the stitch forms loops. If you pull the correct thread, the stitches all come out as you pull.

Chain Stitch

Presser Foot	Regular
Needles	Left, Center, Right
Stitch Length	2 mm to 3 mm
Differential Feed	Normal
Blade Position	Down
Needle Tension	4 to 6
Chain Looper Tension	Chain/Normal
Add Stitch Table	
Disengage Upper Looper	

● Right needle thread
● Chain looper

Chain Stitch Applications

Seaming

With right sides together, place the fabric under the needle. Line up the edge of the fabric with the edge of the needle plate. Serge.

Topstitching

You may want to lengthen your stitch length for topstitching. Place the edge of the fabric under the needle and start to serge. Using two strands of all-purpose thread in the needle gives a heavier look to the topstitching.

Decorative Chaining

To create a decorative chain stitch from the wrong side of the fabric, use an enhancing thread such as Jean Stitch, Pearl Crown Rayon or metallic yarn in the chain looper, with regular serger cone thread in the needle.

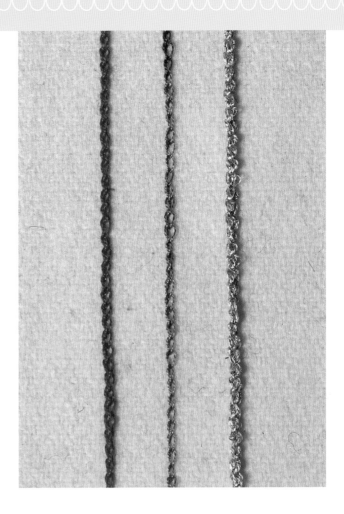

Note from Nancy

 It's also fun to make tassels using decorative thread and the chain stitch. (See page 73 for that technique.)

Basting

Simply lengthen your stitch length and stitch a chain stitch to baste fabrics together. Works well for alterations, too!

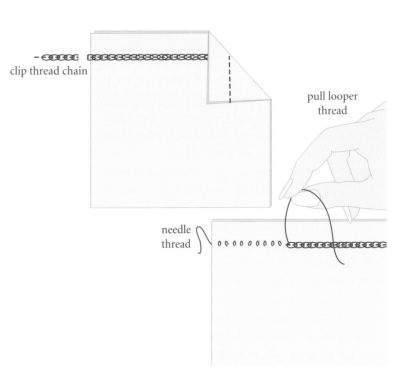

clip thread chain

pull looper thread

needle thread

Note from Nancy

*Pulling the looper thread is the key to unraveling the chain stitch. Start with the **end** of the seam, rather than the beginning of the serged chain stitch. Simply clip the thread chain next to the end of the serging. Separate the two threads on the underside of the fabric with a pin or stiletto. Pull the looper thread toward the chain stitch and the stitches will unravel.*

Overlock/Coverlock Combination Stitches

The following stitch combinations are specific to certain sergers. Check your manual to see if you are able to obtain them and what settings should be used on your serger. As you feel comfortable with your serger and want to learn something new, these would be perfect options for you to try.

4-Thread Combo

This stitch uses the chain stitch (one chain needle and chain looper) and a 2-thread wide or narrow overlock (left or right overlock needle and lower looper with auxiliary looper engaged). It is great for seaming sweater knits. You may also want to set your differential feed between 1.3 and 2 to eliminate stretch distortion.

5-Thread Safety Stitch

This is the most popular and durable of the combination stitches. It uses a 3-thread overlock (left or right overlock needle, upper and lower loopers) and a 2-thread chain stitch (chain needle and chain looper). Many ready-to-wear garments feature this stitch. Another use would be as a decorative border using decorative threads such as Pearl Crown Rayon or Jean Stitch thread in the upper and lower loopers.

6-Thread Stitch

This stitch is also referred to as the Heirloom Hem Finish. It is great for hemming linen napkins or tablecloths. The cover stitch uses the center and right needles and the overlock is a 3-thread rolled hem using the right needle, with upper and lower loopers. The 6-thread stitch could also be used for hemming high loft fleece. In that case, use a right chain needle and chain looper with a 4-thread overlock. Other combinations can be used to create decorative borders.

7-Thread Stitch

A triple cover stitch and a 3-thread wide overlock create a 7-thread stitch, which is primarily used as a reversible decorative border.

8-Thread Stitch

Last but not least is the eighth wonder of the serger world—a triple cover stitch with a 4-thread overlock! Using regular cone thread, this stitch produces a ⅝" seam that is *very* durable for denim, upholstery fabrics and heavy knits. It's a grand stitch for anyone who does a lot of home decorating. The 8-thread stitch can also become a reversible decorative border using decorative threads specified in your instruction manual.

Note from Nancy

Remember that when working with heavy knits, it may be necessary to loosen the pressure on the presser foot. (See page 27.)

Decorative and Top Cover Stitches

Pfaff's newest serger is the ultimate in creativity! This serger stitch variation features up to six decorative threads. The cover stitch is used to couch the decorative threads into position. The seven different stitch programs offer a variety of decorative and top cover stitches using five to 10 threads.

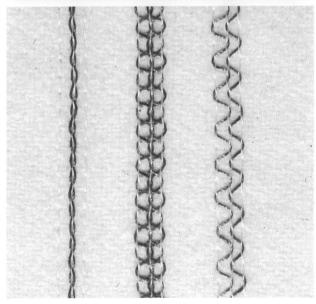

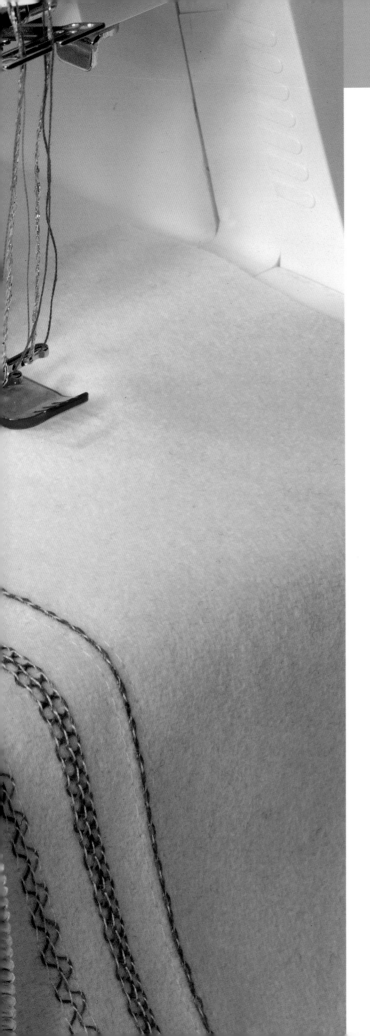

Go—
Serge Ahead—

You've made it!

From basics to beyond your wildest dream, you can explore new-age stitching techniques here. This 2-thread to 10-thread stitch safari is meant to tame the beastly rumors of serging.

Serging Basics

Basic serging techniques start your journey into the serging world with newfound success. Take a few minutes to try some of these basic serging fundamentals. You'll be glad you did.

Securing Stitches—Beginning and End

Some of these security stitches take a little practice. See which ones work best for you.

Locked Beginning

1 Use a 3- or 4-thread overlock stitch with blade engaged.

2 Serge a chain about 2" to 3" long.

3 Take several stitches into the fabric. *(or 1 stitch)* Stop serging, lower the needle and lift the presser foot.

4 Stretch the thread chain out behind the foot carefully to even out the loops. Bring the chain underneath the presser foot and to the right.

5 Lower the presser foot and continue to serge, stitching over the thread chain.

6 Trim off the thread chain with the serger blades and continue serging.

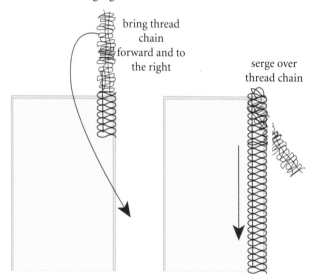

bring thread chain forward and to the right

serge over thread chain

Locked End

1 Serge to the edge of the fabric, but not beyond. Stop with the needles up and lift the presser foot.

2 Insert your finger under the needle threads and pull a small amount of thread "slack" above the needles.

3 Gently pull fabric to the back to clear thread from the stitch fingers.

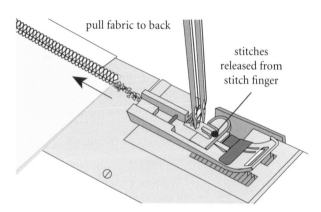

pull fabric to back

stitches released from stitch finger

4 Turn over the fabric so the stitching line is toward the front.

5 Serge over the previous stitches for about 1" before stitching off the fabric edge. Be careful so you don't cut into the previous stitching.

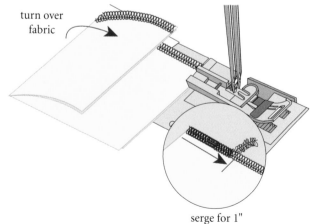

turn over fabric

serge for 1"

Concealed Thread End

To conceal a serged thread beginning or end, simply use a double eyed needle. Insert the thread tail through the eye and slide it under the stitches in the serged seam. Trim off the excess thread tail.

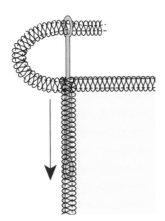

Using a Seam Sealant

Seam sealants can be used at the beginning or end of a seam. These sealants dry clear, but may become brittle if you use too much. The following technique keeps the thread more pliable.

1 Quarter-fold a piece of paper toweling and place it on your ironing board.

2 Place a small drop of seam sealant on the thread edge and place the seam on top of the paper towel.

3 Touch the sealed edge with the tip of your iron. The heat will dry the sealant immediately and the excess will be forced into the paper towel. (Do not use the iron on threads that will melt.) Clip the excess thread.

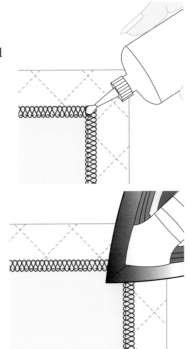

4 If you get any residue build-up on your iron, remove it by placing a small amount of iron cleaner such as Iron-off™ on a paper towel and following package instructions.

Removing Serged Stitches

"Reverse serging" is never fun; however, these few options for removing serged stitches should help you immensely!

Pulling the Needle Threads

1 Clip off the thread tails at each end of the seam.

2 Find the needle threads. (There will be two needle threads for a 4-thread stitch and one for a 3-thread stitch.)

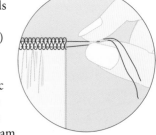

3 Pull the needle threads. This will gather the fabric slightly. Slide the gathers along the fabric until the thread pulls out of the seam.

4 The looper threads now have no anchor threads keeping them in position, so you can pull them freely from the edge of the fabric.

Using a Serger Seam Ripper

The curved blade on this seam ripper protects the seam while you quickly slice the stitches. After the stitches are cut, the remaining threads will pull out easily. Using a serger seam ripper does get a little messy because of all the short threads that are left in the seam!

Note from **Nancy**

Use Sticky Finger mitts or a lint roller to remove the excess trimmed stitches. It works like a charm!

Unraveling a Chain Stitch

It is a simple process to unravel a chain stitch if you pull on the correct thread. You might want to thread your machine with different-colored threads to see which thread in the chain stitch is the needle thread and which is the looper thread when serged. (See page 51.)

Corners

As basic as it may seem to serge corners and angles, when you add an additional element, such as "cutting," it takes a little more practice. Soon you will be serging tablecloths, scarves, napkins, pockets and collars with beautiful edges.

The following corner techniques are generally stitched with a 3- or 4-thread overlock stitch or a rolled hem. It is best to have the blade engaged and trim off a small amount of fabric when serging.

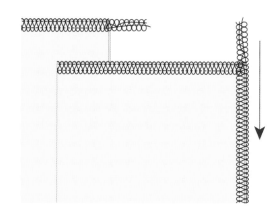

Three-Step Outside Corners

1 Serge along one edge and trim thread leaving a 2" to 3" thread chain.

2 Pivot the fabric and serge the adjacent edge, trimming off the short chain from the first edge as you serge.

3 Seal or lock the remaining thread tail using one of the methods on page 57. Once the thread tail is sealed or locked, the excess can be trimmed.

This quick method is great for napkins!

Continuous Outside Corners
This takes a little more thought!

1 Stitch to the end of the corner, but not beyond.

2 Stop with the needles up and raise the presser foot.

3 Pull a small amount of thread just above the needles. This "thread slack" will release stitches from the stitch finger. (See page 56.)

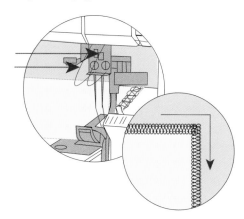

4 Pivot the fabric, lining up the adjacent side.

5 To tighten the needle threads, gently pull them taut just before the tension guides.

6 Lower the presser foot and continue serging.

Inside Corners

1 Serge the first edge, stopping about 1" away from inside corner. To obtain a more square corner, clip diagonally ⅛" from corner. Be careful not to clip too deep or you will have a hole in the corner of the fabric.

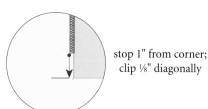

stop 1" from corner; clip ⅛" diagonally

2 Lower needles to secure the fabric. Raise the presser foot.

3 When you straighten the cut edge, several small pleats will form in the corner to the left of the presser foot. Lower the presser foot and continue to serge the edge.

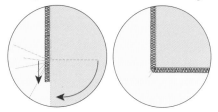

Note from Nancy

Inner corners can be difficult to serge. Sometimes, it is much easier to use your sewing machine in tandem with your serger to stitch the frustrating areas.

Wrapped Corners

When serging, it is impossible to pivot at corners in the traditional way. Wrapped corners eliminate bulk from a collar by serging the outer edges in a few easy steps. This is destined to become one of your favorite techniques!

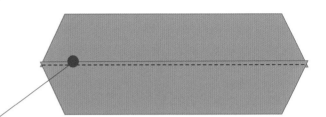

1 Fuse interfacing to the wrong sides of both collars according to the manufacturer's instructions.

2 With right sides together, pin the collars along the unnotched edges. Serge from end to end.

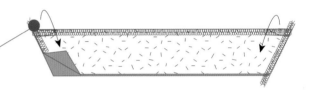

3 Press the seam flat and then toward the under-collar.

4 Understitch with a straight stitch on a conventional machine, if desired.

5 Fold the collar along the seam with right sides together. Seam allowances will wrap toward the under-collar. Serge from the fold to the neckline edge on each end of the collar.

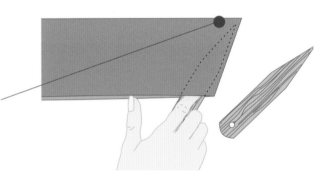

6 Press the seams flat.

7 Apply a drop of seam sealant; let dry. Then trim thread tails.

8 Turn the collar right side out. Use a Bamboo Pointer & Creaser to help shape the point of the collar.

Stabilized Seams

Seams such as shoulder seams that tend to stretch should be stabilized before serging. *A 4-thread overlock is best for stabilizing seams.*

1 Place fabrics right sides together with the front on top.

2 Put a stabilizing tape such as twill tape, ribbon or interfacing over the seamline. (See page 32.)

3 Serge the seam through all layers, guiding the needle on the seamline.

Note from Nancy

Some serger feet have a special groove to aid in guiding the stabilizer tape. Check your manual to see if you have this feature.

Circular Edges

Inside circular edge—not exposed
(e.g., ribbing on a neckline)

1   Raise the presser foot and needles.

2   Insert the fabric, aligning the fabric with the left side of the upper blade.

3   Lower the presser foot and begin to serge. Move the fabric slowly to the *left* in front of the foot for an inside curve.

4   Stitch off the edge of the fabric at the end of the circle. Be careful not to cut the threads you serged previously!

5   Use seam sealant to seal the end; trim the thread tail when dry.

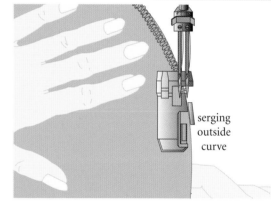

serging
inside
curve

Note from Nancy

As you are stitching keep an eye on the cutting blade and not the needles, to make sure that if you trim, you remove the same amount all around the circle.

Outside circular edge —not exposed
(e.g., inside seam on a round pillow)
Use the same procedure as the inside curve, except move fabric slowly to the *right* in front of the foot.

serging
outside
curve

Outside circular edge with decorative serging— exposed (e.g., round tablecloth)
1   Use a shorter stitch length on outside edges for better thread coverage and more uniform stitches.

2   Cut a "starting gate" along the circular edge by cutting out a ¼" x 2" section along the outer edge.

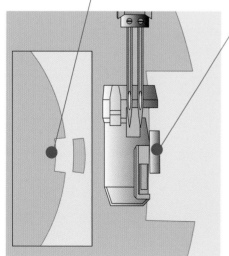

3   Place the serger foot in the starting gate, aligning the blade area next to the cutout section.

4   Serge along the edge, trimming off the ¼" seam allowance.

5   At the end of the circle, serge over several of the beginning stitches to secure the threads. Release threads from the stitch finger; clip threads.

6   Apply a seam sealant to the thread ends. After the sealant is dry, clip the thread ends.

Note from Nancy

Stitch quality generally is better if a small amount of fabric is trimmed away, rather than serging precisely along a cut edge.

Easing/Gathering

Differential Feed Gathering

When the differential feed is set at a larger number, the front feed dog will move faster than the back feed dog. This results in gathering the fabric. If the fabric isn't gathered enough, pull the needle threads to gather more. If the fabric is gathered too much, simply ease out the excess gathering by gently sliding your fingers across the stitching.

- Use a 4-thread overlock for this type of gathering on lightweight fabric.

- Set the stitch width at the widest setting and the stitch length at the longest setting.

- Adjust the differential feed to approximately 2.

- Use either the locked or unlocked blade setting.

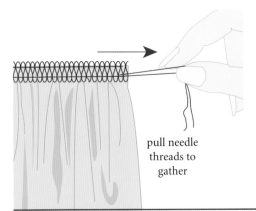

pull needle
threads to
gather

Note from Nancy

This is a wonderful serger technique to use when "easing in" a sleeve cap and finishing edges at the same time. Start serging with normal 4-thread settings. When you approach a notch, adjust settings for gathering. (Change length, width and differential feed settings.) Serge from notch to double-notch on the sleeve cap using the gathering settings. Then return your stitch length, width and differential feed to normal settings. Adjust gathers to fit the sleeve.

Tension Gathering

If your machine doesn't have the differential feed feature, try "tension gathering."

- Use the longest and widest stitch.

- Tighten your needle tensions.

Note from Nancy

Sometimes, it helps to decrease the presser foot pressure by turning the pressure knob counterclockwise a small amount. This adjustment will encourage the fabric to gather.

Filler Cord Gathering

Serge over a cord and pull it to gather the edge of heavier fabrics.

- Use a filler cord such as Buttonhole Twist or Gimp. As an option, use elastic cording as the filler cord to build stretch into the gathered edge.
- Use left needle only and normal 3-thread settings.

1 Place a knot in the filler cord.

2 Insert the cord over the front of the presser foot and under the back (between the needle and the blades)

3 Serge over the cord, being careful not to cut it!

4 Hold onto the knot and pull slightly as you serge to begin the gathering process.

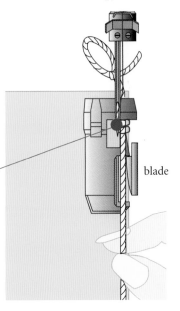

blade

Beyond the Basics

Easy to accomplish, yet decorative and a bit out of the ordinary—those are the techniques featured next. On the following pages, we will explore decorative overlock, rolled edge, flatlock, cover stitch and chain stitch options. Pick your favorites and get creative!

Decorative Overlock Options

Puffing

This 4-thread heirloom technique creates a puffed strip of trim that is gathered on both edges and can be inserted into a garment or pillow.

1. Set a long stitch length and stitch width.

2. Set differential feed to the largest number.

3. Use a lightweight fabric and cut the insertion strip the desired width by twice the length needed.

4. Use one of the 4-thread serger techniques on page 61 to gather each long edge.

5. Distribute gathers evenly and insert into project.

Scalloped Edge

A scalloped edge can be created by using your serger and a conventional sewing machine in tandem. It's a dainty decorative edge that is perfect for receiving blankets, lingerie and other lightweight garments.

1. Set up the serger for a narrow 3-thread overlock or rolled hem stitch.

2. Use a narrow stitch width and a satin stitch length approximately 1 mm to 2 mm.

3. Use a lightweight decorative thread in the loopers and regular thread to coordinate with your project in the needle.

4. Serge the edges to be scalloped.

5. Set up your conventional machine for a reversed (mirror-imaged) blind hem or a shell stitch. Such stitch settings will allow you to sew with your fabric to the left of the machine needle, making it easier to control the bulk.

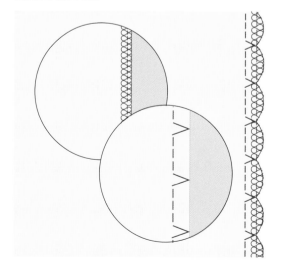

Serger Twists

Serger twists are created by using different colors of thread in the upper and lower loopers. Stitch several rows of narrow 3-thread overlock. Then using a conventional sewing machine, stitch through adjacent serged rows in alternating directions. The stitching creates a twisted appearance to the serging.

1   Adjust the serger for a narrow 3-thread overlock using the right needle, a narrow to normal stitch width and a 1.5 stitch length.

2   Thread the needle and lower looper with thread coordinating with your fabric. Thread the upper looper with a contrasting thread color.

3   If possible, disengage the blade so it will not cut the fabric. Or, guide the fabric slightly away from the blade.

4   Mark lines ¾" apart on the fabric with a water-soluble fabric marker.

5   Fold and serge along all marked lines in the same direction. Press all stitching in the same direction.

6   Mark lines 1" apart perpendicular to the serged lines.

7   Using a conventional sewing machine, straight stitch along the marked lines, alternating stitching direction on each row.

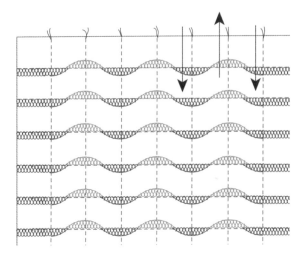

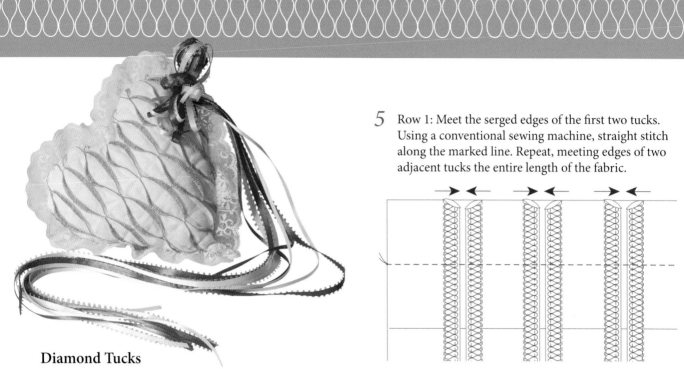

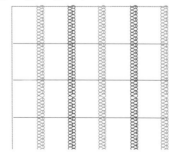

Diamond Tucks

Diamond tucks are accomplished in much the same way as the serger twists, except the serging direction is alternated and conventional stitching is also varied. The tucks created have a smocked appeal. This is a fun serger decoration for pillows and other home décor, as well as for insertions into the yokes or other areas on a garment.

1　Set up the serger the same as for "Serger Twists," page 63.

2　Mark lines on the fabric ¾" apart.

3　Fold and serge on all marked lines, alternating serging direction on each row. Press tucks flat in either direction.

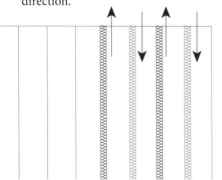

4　Mark lines 1" apart perpendicular to the serged lines.

5　Row 1: Meet the serged edges of the first two tucks. Using a conventional sewing machine, straight stitch along the marked line. Repeat, meeting edges of two adjacent tucks the entire length of the fabric.

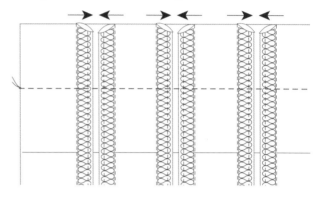

6　Row 2: Fold the first tuck outward. Meet serged edges of the next two tucks and continue stitching. Repeat for the entire length, always meeting edges of the next two adjacent tucks.

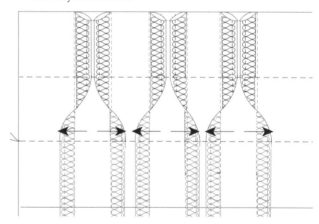

7　Alternate Row 1 and Row 2 until all lines have been stitched.

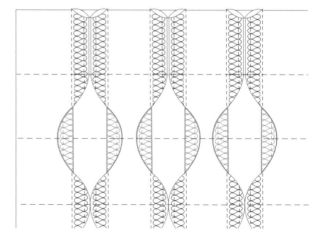

Serge and Fuse Seams

Add color and detail by combining a basic 3-thread overlock stitch, decorative thread, fusible thread and exposed seams. The seams are serged and pressed flat—and they stay flat because of a specialty fusible thread in the lower looper.

Note from **Nancy**

Fusible thread is a polyester thread that is twisted with a heat-activated fusible fiber, making it sensitive to heat and moisture. The pliable bond withstands both washing and dry cleaning. On a serger, fusible thread is generally used in the lower looper.

1 Set up the serger for a 3-thread overlock using the left needle.

2 Use the widest width and a narrow length (1 mm to 2.5 mm).

3 Slightly loosen the upper looper tension and slightly tighten the lower looper tension.

To Fuse Decorative Facing Edges:

1 Stitch outer edge, right side up, using serger cone thread in the needle, decorative thread in the upper looper and fusible thread in the lower looper.

2 Attach facing to garment, meeting right side of facing to wrong side of garment.

3 Press facing to right side of garment. Fuse facing in place.

To Serge and Fuse Decorative Seams:

1 Use serger cone thread in the needle, decorative thread in the upper looper and fusible thread in the lower looper.

2 Place wrong sides together and serge seams so the left needle stitches at the ⅝" seamline. **This is very important.** If the needle is not at the seamline, the finished garment will be larger than expected.

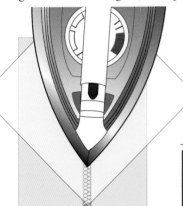

3 The blades should be engaged, as the remainder of the seam allowance will be trimmed away.

4 Finger press seam allowance to one side. (Fusible side must be on the underside.)

5 Cover seam with a press cloth and steam to bond the seam allowance to the right side of the garment.

Note from **Nancy**

Always check the iron temperature on a scrap of fabric before doing the actual fusing. Remember, you're working on the right side of the fabric. If the iron is too hot, you could melt or change the appearance of the decorative thread and ruin the entire garment.

Decorative Rolled Edge Options

Lettuce Edges

The lettuce edge is a variation of the rolled edge. Stretch the edge as you serge to get a "funky" curled look. It works great on knit ribbed necklines and cuffs, as well as hems on lightweight knit shirts and trim on Lycra® swimsuits and activewear.

Pintucks

Serger pintucks are an heirloom variation of the rolled edge. Lightweight fabrics, such as batiste, work very well for this technique. On some models, you may need to attach a pintuck foot or rolled edge foot for best results. Consult your instruction manual.

1 Adjust serger for a 3-thread rolled edge.

2 Use a narrow width and a rolled hem length setting of 1.5 mm.

3 Lock or disengage the cutting blade, if possible.

4 Thread needle and lower looper with cone thread and upper looper with decorative rayon, if desired.

5 Mark lines ¾" apart.

6 Fold and press along each marked line. Stitch pintucks.

7 Press all tucks in the same direction, with upper looper thread on top.

1 Set up the serger up for a 3-thread rolled edge.

2 Use Woolly Nylon in the loopers and regular cone thread in the needle for an attractive lettuce edge.

3 Use a normal width and a rolled hem length setting of 1 to 2.

4 Lock or disengage the cutting blade, if possible.

5 Guide the fabric along the right edge of the presser foot.

6 Stretch the ribbing an equal amount from front and back while serging. It also helps to lower the differential feed, if available, to about 0.6.

7 Serge at a slow to moderate speed.

Note from **Nancy**

If you want the edge to curl a bit more, gently stretch and release the fabric edge after serging.

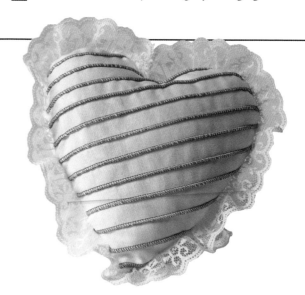

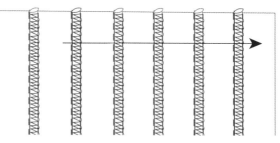

Rolled Edge Piping

This lightweight piping is simple to create using Seams Great®, a bias-cut nylon. You can customize the color to coordinate with your project by simply changing threads.

1 Set up the serger for a 3-thread rolled edge.

2 Use a wide width and a rolled hem length setting of 2 mm.

3 Serge with the blade unlocked (engaged).

4 Thread the upper and lower loopers with Woolly Nylon thread and the needle with coordinating cone thread.

5 Guide the Seams Great® along the edge of the needle plate, trimming excess Seams Great® as you serge.

6 For heavier piping, change the stitch length to 1 mm and serge again over previous stitching.

Decorative Flatlock Options

Flatlock Weaving

Create lovely trim and decorative stitching using a 2-thread flatlock ladder stitch and weaving beads, ribbon, yarn and trims through it. It's as unique as the designer!

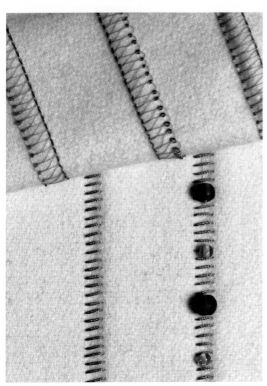

Beads on Ladder Stitch

1 Set up the serger for a 2-thread right needle flatlock stitch as indicated in your instruction manual.

2 Use a medium stitch width and a 3.5 mm stitch length.

3 Lock or disengage the cutting blade, if possible.

4 Engage the 2-Thread Converter.

5 Set the differential feed at normal to 1.3.

6 Serge from the wrong side of the fabric with buttonhole twist or other heavy thread in a topstitching needle. This will give you a ladder stitch on the right side of the fabric.

7 Thread a large-eyed needle with buttonhole twist thread. Go under four of the ladder stitches, then through a bead. Skip two to four stitches (depending on the length of the bead). Repeat under four, add bead, etc.

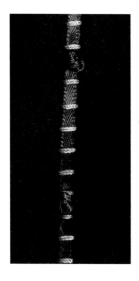

Ribbon Knots on Ladder Stitch

1. Use a 2-thread wide stitch with the same threads as "Beads on Ladder Stitch," page 67.

2. Use the left needle.

3. Adjust serger as for "Beads on Ladder Stitch," page 67, except set stitch width at the widest setting.

4. Thread ribbon under four or eight stitches. Tie a knot or double knot. Repeat.

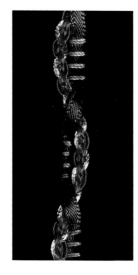

Braiding on Ladder Stitch

1. Use the same settings as "Ribbon Knots on Ladder Stitch," at left. Thread ⅛" ribbon under four stitches then over four stitches. Repeat.

2. Weave braid in and out of the ribbon, alternating from side to side.

Flatlock Blanket Stitch

The flatlock blanket stitch is perfect for a single layer of fleece or wool. It is a decorative edge finish created with a 2-thread flatlock and clear wash-away stabilizer.

1. Set up the serger for a 2-thread left needle flatlock as indicated in your instruction manual.

2. On some machines, you will need to thread the needle thread through the upper looper thread guides. Check your instruction manual.

3. Use the widest stitch width and a 4 mm stitch length.

4. Lock or disengage the cutting blade, if possible.

5. Engage the 2-Thread Converter.

6. Set the differential feed at normal to 1.5.

7. Use regular cone thread in the lower looper and a decorative thread in the needle, such as Sulky® 12 wt. Cotton, Jean Stitch thread or Decor 6.

8. Insert a topstitching needle (Size 90/14). A topstitching needle keeps thread shredding to a minimum and is much easier to thread because of the large eye.

9. Place a layer of clear wash-away stabilizer, such as Sulky® Ultra Solvy™ or two layers of Wash-Away, on (top) right side of fabric.

10. Serge slowly to achieve even stitches through the layer of wash-away stabilizer and lofty fabric.

11. Pull the stabilizer away from the stitches, off the edge of the lofty fabric. The decorative thread will form a blanket stitch on the edge of the fabric.

12. Gently tear away excess stabilizer.

standard needle   topstitching needle

Flatlocked Lace and Ribbon

Attach lace and narrow ribbon at the same time as you stitch this 2-thread flatlock decorative stitch.

1 Set up the serger for a 2-thread right needle flatlock stitch as indicated in your instruction manual.

2 Use a medium stitch width and a 3 mm stitch length.

3 Lock or disengage cutting blade, if possible.

4 Engage the 2-Thread Converter.

5 Set the differential feed at normal to 0.6.

6 Use regular cone thread matching the fabric in the needle.

7 Use rayon thread matching the ribbon in the lower looper.

8 Mark lines on fabric approximately 1" apart.

9 Fold the fabric on marked line, wrong sides together.

10 Place the ribbon to the right of the needle, over the front of the presser foot and under the back. Leave approximately a 1" tail behind the back of the foot.

11 Place the straight edge of the lace trim on the edge of fabric, right side facing up.

12 Position the fabric and lace under the presser foot. Take two to three stitches by turning the hand wheel, making sure the needle does not catch the ribbon. Sew slowly over the ribbon. Gently pull the stitches flat when sewing is complete. Repeat for remaining rows.

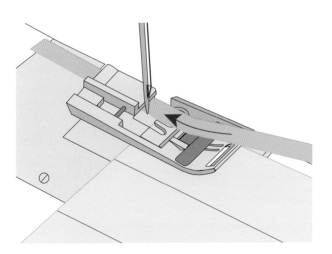

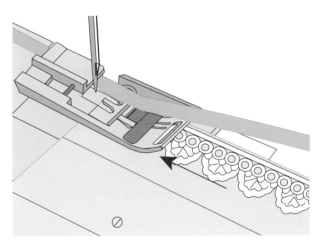

Flatlock Patchwork

Flatlock patchwork can be primarily functional using all-purpose cone threads. Or, add elegance to this nonbulky seam design by using decorative threads. Either way, your patchwork will be decoratively enhanced!

1   Cut 2½"-wide strips of two coordinating fabrics. The number and length will vary, depending on the desired amount of patchwork.

2   Set up the serger for a 2-thread flatlock, using the right needle for a narrow stitch or the left needle for a wide stitch. Consult your instruction manual for settings appropriate for your serger.

3   Select all-purpose threads for functional flatlocking or decorative threads for a more elegant look. Metallic or other decorative thread works well in the needle, with rayon thread in the lower looper.

4   Meet strips, wrong sides together, alternating fabrics.

5   Flatlock the strips, guiding fabrics about ⅛" away from the blade so none of the fabric is trimmed away. Loop stitches will be visible on the right sides of the fabric.

6   Flatten the strips and subcut them into 2½" sections.

7   Rotate alternate sections 180 degrees to form a patchwork design. Join sections by flatlocking, right sides together. On this seam, ladder stitches will be visible on the right side of the fabric.

8   Join as many sections as needed for the project.

9   Serge around the outer edges with an overlock or rolled edge to complete the patchwork.

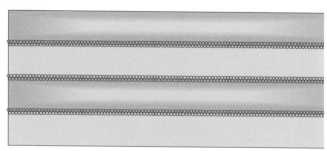

flatlock strips together

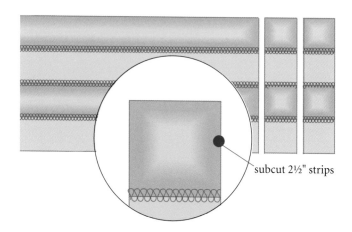

subcut 2½" strips

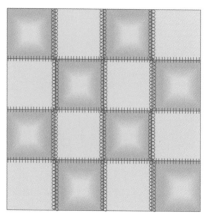

Cover Stitch Options

Cover Stitch Shadow Work

The delicate shadow work created with this stitch is enhanced by using a transparent fabric like batiste or organdy so the chain looper thread is visible, shadowing through the fabric.

1 Adjust the serger for a two-needle wide cover stitch as indicated in your instruction manual, using a normal stitch width and a 1.5 mm to 3 mm stitch length (depending on thread used).

2 Disengage blade and upper looper.

3 Attach sewing table.

4 Thread both needles and the chain looper with thread contrasting with the fabric. For greatest contrast, thread the chain looper with Woolly Nylon or Pearl Cotton thread. Test stitching; check thread coverage.

5 Mark stitching lines on transparent fabric.

6 Cover stitch along all lines.

7 Back the fabric with a layer of similarly colored cotton fabric to make the stitching more prominent.

Cover Stitch Patchwork

Make a sheer patchwork such as the one featured below or use durable cotton fabrics to create your one-of-a-kind creation. Fusible patchwork enhanced with a cover stitch gives a totally new look to this serger sensation.

For more specific instructions for the Organza Scarf, see pages 96 and 97.

1 Adjust the serger the same as in step 1 of Cover Stitch Shadow Work above.

2 Disengage blade and upper looper.

3 Attach sewing table.

4 Thread chain looper and needles with regular cone thread or a decorative thread, such as rayon embroidery thread.

5 Back wrong sides of patchwork squares and rectangles with lightweight paper-backed fusible web, following manufacturer's instructions.

6 Remove paper backing, arrange and fuse the patchwork pieces to the main fabric.

7 Serge over each edge of the patchwork with a cover stitch. Serge all lengthwise edges first and then the crosswise edges.

8 Apply seam sealant to serged ends to keep them from raveling.

9 Finish project as desired.

Cover Stitch Braid/Fringe Trim

Serge decorative braid/fringe trim for garments and home decorating projects. It's fun to serge and making braid yourself makes it truly unique. Start with a loosely woven fabric that fringes well and add a few serging skills.

1 Set up the machine for a narrow cover stitch hem following your instruction manual.
- Use all-purpose cone thread to coordinate with fabric in the needles.
- Use Jean Stitch or Pearl Crown Rayon thread in the chain looper.

2 Cut a strip of loosely woven fabric approximately 3½" wide.

3 Align ½" Stay-Tape™ down the center of the fabric (wrong side), following a woven plaid line in the fabric, if available.

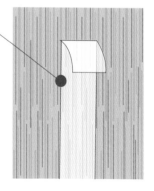

4 Guide left needle along left edge of Stay-Tape™ and serge a narrow cover stitch. Turn fabric around and serge down the opposite side of the trim in the same manner.

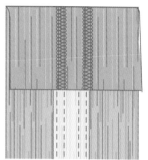

5 Add a third row of narrow cover stitch between the first two rows. We used a different color for better visibility.

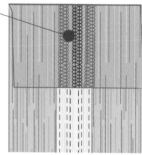

6 Change serger to a wide cover stitch.

7 Center and serge a wide cover stitch down the middle of the Stay-Tape™ (over the third row of narrow cover stitching).

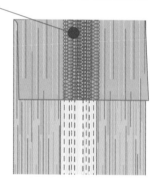

8 Trim one edge of the fabric to the desired fringe length (usually ¾" to 1").

9 Trim opposite edge of fabric to the width of the "braid" (approximately ½") for a hem.

10 Ravel the fringe side of the fabric and press under the braid hem on the opposite side.

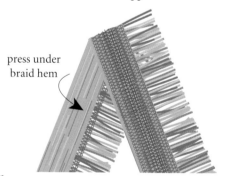

press under braid hem

11 Pin and baste braid trim in place on garment or other project. Edgestitch with sewing machine.

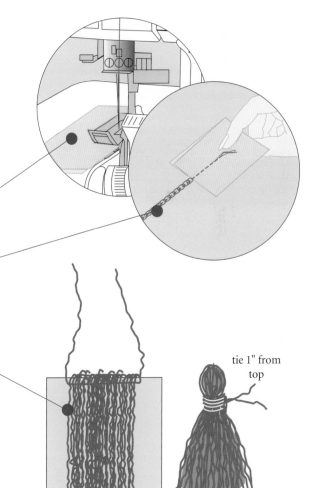

Chain Stitch Tassels

Create lovely tassels to coordinate with your project. Experiment with various types of threads for unique tassels. Add a touch of class to your home décor and accessory ideas.

1   Adjust the serger for a center needle chain stitch as indicated in your instruction manual, using a 2 mm to 4 mm stitch length.

2   Disengage blade and upper looper.

3   Attach sewing table.

4   Use rayon or metallic thread in the needle to coordinate with the looper thread.

5   Use rayon, metallic, Candlelight, Designer 6 or Pearl Crown thread in the chain looper.

6   Fold a piece of cotton fabric in half and position it under the needle. It is usually necessary to start a chain or cover stitch on an anchor cloth. (See page 46.)

7   Serge beyond the fabric to form a thread chain. Serge about 20 to 22 yards for each tassel.

On some chain/cover stitch sergers the chain stitch needs to be serged with fabric underneath in order to form a stitch.

8   When finished, remove the thread chain from the machine and wrap it around a 4" square of cardboard. The more thread chain you use, the larger the tassel will be.

9   Reserve two 9" pieces of chain. Use one to tie the threads at the top and form a loop. Clip threads at the tassel end. Use the second piece of chain to tie the tassel together about 1" from the top.

tie 1" from top

Specialty Serger Feet

Specialty serger feet are definitely helpful; each serves a particular purpose. Although you may not find all of these feet essential when you first start serging, as you gain confidence, you'll undoubtedly want to purchase those that will complement the projects you plan to do.

Keep in mind that serger feet vary in appearance from one company to the next, so the foot for your machine may look slightly different than the one shown in this book. Check your instruction manual to see which feet are available for your serger and the specific details for using them.

Ruffling/Shirring Foot

The main advantage of the ruffling foot is being able to serge two pieces of fabric together, gathering only one layer. There are two slots for feeding fabric. One layer of fabric is inserted in the top slot and a second layer is inserted in the bottom under the spring tension bar. Determine the length of the ruffle strip by measuring the area to which it will be attached and multiply by two. Most ruffling feet gather at a 2:1 ratio, but the ratio varies with the weight of the fabric. Always cut the strip slightly longer than needed to allow for any slight deviations in the gathering ratio and to provide enough fabric for joining the two ends of the ruffled strip.

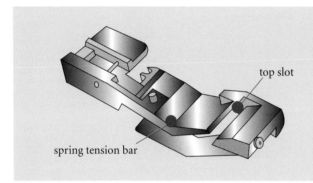

top slot

spring tension bar

Stitch: 4-Thread Overlock
Needles: Right and Left
Width: Normal to Widest
Length: 4 mm
Differential Feed: 2 (tightest setting)
Blade Position: Unlocked (engaged)
Fabric: Lightweight
Presser Foot: Ruffling/Shirring Foot

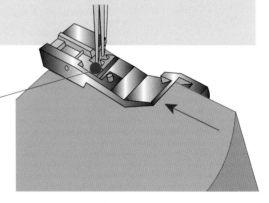

The serger settings are the same as those for gathering with a 4-thread overlock. (See page 61.)

1 Raise the presser foot. Place fabric you are attaching to the ruffle right side down in the top slot of the ruffling foot. Make sure the fabric is straight and flat. Place the needles down into the fabric to secure it.

2 Place the fabric you are ruffling right side up under the bottom of the presser foot. Advance the fabric as far back to the needles as possible and lower the presser foot.

3 Take several stitches by turning the hand wheel to catch both fabrics.

4 Serge slowly, guiding the top fabric with your left hand and the bottom fabric with your right hand.

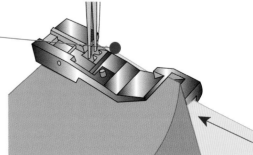

Elastic Foot

The elastic foot stretches and attaches the elastic to fit a project as the serger trims the excess fabric. This foot is a great timesaver, especially with narrow elastic that is more difficult to attach with other methods. Some elastic feet have an additional hole to insert corded elastic, fishing line or fine wire, which gives you many decorative options.

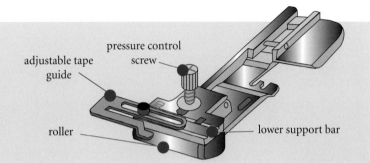

Stitch: 4-Thread Overlock
Needles: Right and Left
Width: Normal
Length: 4 mm
Differential Feed: 2 (tightest setting)
Blade Position: Locked (disengaged)
Presser Foot: Elastic Foot

Elastic Insertion

1. Set up your serger for a 4-thread overlock. A cover stitch can also be used with some elastic feet. Check your instruction manual if you have the cover stitch on your machine. Also make sure to check the instructions for your elastic foot.

2. Loosen the pressure control screw on the top of the foot, if necessary, so the elastic can be placed between the roller (brake) and the lower support bar.

3. Insert elastic and slide it to the back of and under the foot.

4. Tighten the pressure control screw slightly.

5. Attach the elastic foot to the serger.

6. Stitch a sample and adjust the pressure control screw as necessary for the desired effect. Tighten the screw to add more elasticity to the fabric. Loosen the screw for less elasticity.

Note from **Nancy**

■ *It is much easier to insert the elastic in the foot before placing the foot on the serger.*

Fishing Line and Wire Insertion

Add fishing line to make scalloped ruffles on sheer fabric like bridal tulle, or add wire to the serged edges of wire-edged ribbons. (See pages 99 and 100.) Check your instruction manual for directions specific to your serger.

Stitch: 3-Thread Rolled Edge
Needle: Right
Width: Normal to Wide
Length: 1 mm to 1.5 mm (rolled hem setting)
Differential Feed: Normal to 0.6
Blade Position: Unlocked (engaged)
Presser Foot: Elastic Foot

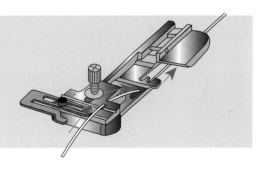

Beading Foot

Pearl Available

Attach prestrung pearls to the edge of a veil, beaded couching on pillow tops or make your own cording and couch it on a crazy patch pillow or purse. The following instructions feature a 3-thread rolled edge, but your instruction manual may also suggest a narrow flatlock stitch. This foot has many creative options!

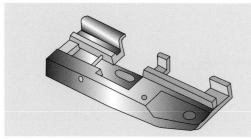

Stitch: 3-Thread Rolled Edge
Needle: Right
Width: Narrow
Rolled Hem Length: 2 mm to 4 mm (varies with size of beads or braid)
Differential Feed: .06 to Normal
Blade Position: Locked or Unlocked
Presser Foot: Beading Foot

1 Place prestrung beads or braid in the channel on top of the beading foot.

2 Guide the beads or braid past the right side of the needle and under the back of the beading foot.

3 Leave a 1" to 2" tail behind the presser foot so you have something to hold on to.

4 Take the first few stitches by turning the hand wheel.

5 Once the beads or braid are secure, serge very slowly so you don't break a bead or a needle!

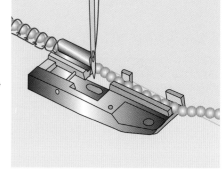

Cording Foot

Piping Available

Many people confuse the beading foot and the cording foot. The beading foot has a channel on **top** of the foot and the beading feeds to the right of the needle. The cording foot has a groove on the **bottom** of the foot and the cording feeds to the left of the needle. The cording foot allows piping or trims to be attached between two layers of fabric in one operation. Choose the size foot that corresponds to the size of your cording. From making and attaching piping to inserting a zipper, the cording foot is a home décor necessity!

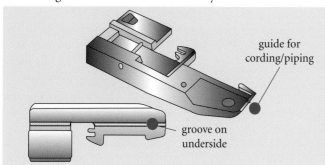

guide for cording/piping

groove on underside

Stitch: 4-Thread Overlock
Needles: Right and Left
Width: Normal to Widest
Length: Normal to Longest
Differential Feed: Normal
Blade Position: Unlocked (engaged)
Presser Foot: Cording Foot (3 mm or 5 mm; depends on size of cording)

Sandwich the piping between two layers of fabric that are right sides together, with the raw edge of the piping facing the blades. Piping will guide in the groove of the cording foot as you serge the seam. Voila! It's an easy one step to attach piping from start to finish!

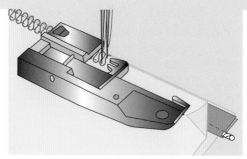

guide piping in groove

Blind Hem Foot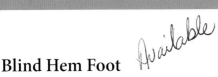

Hemming is the forté of the blind hem foot, but it can also be used to add some creative accents as in decorative flatlocking. The blind hem foot allows you to precisely guide the fabric so rows of flatlocking remain absolutely straight.

Stitch: 2- or 3-Thread Flatlock
Needle: Right
Width: Normal
Length: 4 mm
Differential Feed: Normal to 1.3
Blade Position: Unlocked (engaged)
Subsidiary Looper: Engaged for 2-Thread Flatlock Only
Presser Foot: Blind Hem Foot

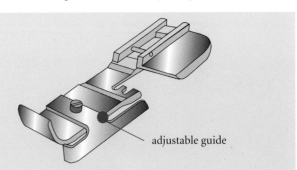

adjustable guide

Note from Nancy

Check your instruction manual for setup using this foot, as some manufacturers suggest using a rolled hem, rather than a flatlock.

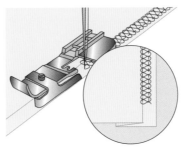

1 Fold hem to the wrong side of the fabric and pin in place, pinning parallel and close to the fold.

2 Fold the fabric back on itself, leaving at least ¼" of the hem extending beyond the fold.

3 Place the fold of the hem under the foot and begin sewing, barely catching the fold with the needle and trimming the extending hem.

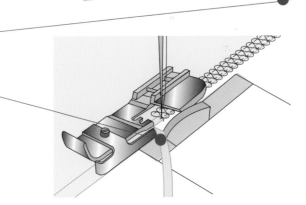

4 The adjustable guide to the right of the foot is essential in determining "bite" of the stitch. Adjust guide on the foot by loosening the screw and sliding the guide left or right, moving the guide closer to or farther away from the needle. If too much thread shows on the right side of the garment, move the guide farther away from the needle (to the right). If the needle thread doesn't catch the hem, move the guide closer to the needle (to the left). A simple adjustment for fantastic results!

5 Pull stitches flat and press when hem is complete.

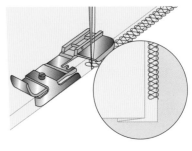

needle bites too deeply
move guide to right

needle does not catch fold
move guide to left

Lace Foot

Create a small heirloom type seam for sewing lace and trims to your garment. Perfectly attached lace is easy using the guide on this specialty foot. This is also a great foot to use for attaching ribbon with a cover stitch or triple cover stitch (three needles).

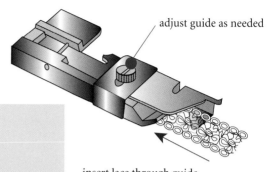

adjust guide as needed

insert lace through guide and under foot

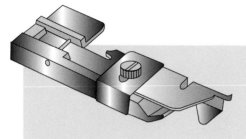

Stitch: Rolled Hem, 3- or 4-Thread Overlock, 2-Thread Flatlock or Cover Stitch. (Select a stitch appropriate for the fabric you are using. Check your instruction manual for specific setup.)
Presser Foot: Lace Foot

Pintuck Foot

A pintuck foot isn't necessary with most 3/4-thread sergers, but if you are using a cover stitch to create the pintucks or corded pintucks, it is an absolute necessity. There are usually two or three parts to this versatile foot.

Stitch: Narrow Cover Stitch (See your instruction manual.)
Stitch Width: Normal
Stitch Length: 3 mm
Differential Feed: Normal to 0.6 (for finer fabrics)
Blade Position: Locked (disengaged)
Presser Foot: Pintuck Foot

groove

One of the attachments guides cording to the foot so it follows the groove under the pintuck foot for a great-looking corded pintuck. The fabric will be guided under the presser foot and over the cord.

If you are stitching regular pintucks with the cover stitch, a "rod" is added to increase the depth of the pintuck.

The pintuck foot is helpful because the regular presser foot of a cover stitch machine tends to be rather wide, making it challenging to position narrow pintucks.

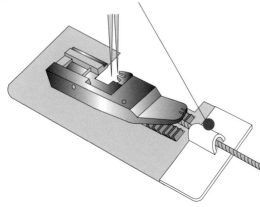

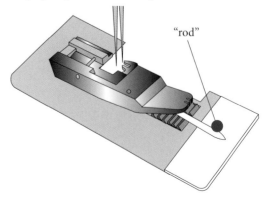

"rod"

Belt Loop Binder Attachment

This attachment makes great belt loops that can be used for garments and other craft projects.

Stitch: Wide or Triple Cover Stitch
Length: 3 mm to 4 mm
Blade Position: Locked (disengaged)
Upper Looper: Down
Presser Foot: Regular Presser Foot

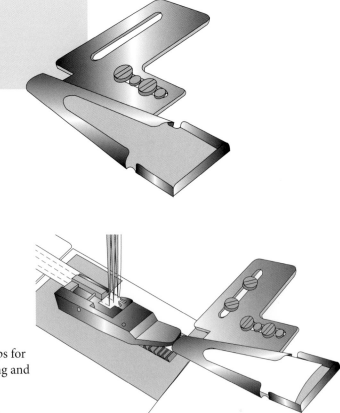

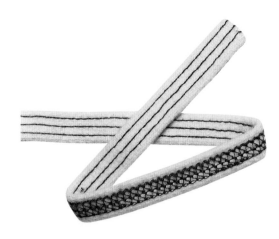

1   Cut bias strips. (⅞" strips for ¾" binder and 1⅝" strips for 1½" binder). Allow 3" to 4" extra bias at the beginning and end of the strip for ease of use.

2   Feed the bias strip into the attachment with right side up.

3   Take the first three to four stitches by turning the hand wheel to secure.

4   Test stitching before starting the actual project.

Note from Nancy

Attachments are also available for single- and double-fold bias binding. Check with your dealer for other attachments to make your serging experience more enjoyable.

Hemmer Attachment

Chain/cover stitch hemmer attachments are available in several different sizes. The most common sizes are ¼" and ½".

Check your instruction manual to see which stitch is recommended for each hemmer. The narrow hemmer usually requires a chain stitch and the larger hemmers generally can use a chain or cover stitch. Settings are quite similar for each stitch.

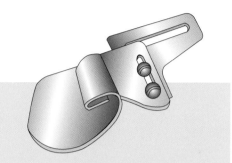

Stitch: Chain Stitch
Stitch Length: 3 mm to 4 mm
Differential Feed: Normal
Upper Looper: Disengaged
Blade Position: Locked (disengaged)
Sewing Table: In Position
Needle Tension: 4 to 6
Chain Looper Tension: Tighten

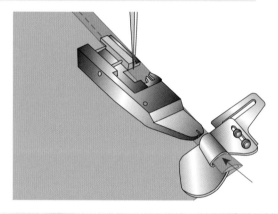

1 Press a narrow ¼" hem to the wrong side of the fabric.

2 Raise the presser foot and slide the fabric into the hemmer, making sure it rolls around the attachment.

3 Lower the presser foot and take a few stitches by hand to secure the end. Keep the fabric turned under as you sew, guiding the fabric slightly to the left. Sew at a steady speed to roll the fabric consistently.

Feller Attachment

A feller attachment works in much the same way as a hemmer attachment. The main difference is that the hemmer turns the fabric twice and the feller turns it once. The feller relies on the looper stitch to finish the raw hem edge as you stitch from the right side of the fabric. The hemmer stitches from the wrong side of the fabric and turns the hem to a clean finish before stitching. The settings for both attachments are very similar. Check your instruction manual for details and settings for the various size attachments.

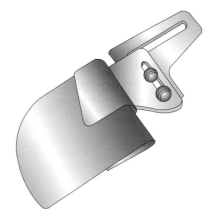

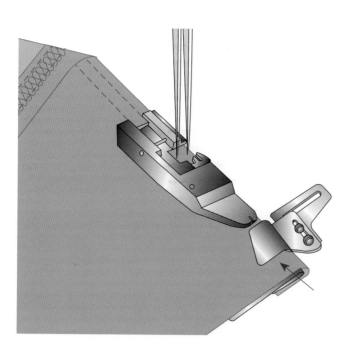

1 Press hem to the wrong side of the fabric.

2 Raise the presser foot and slide the fabric into the feller, making sure it rolls around the attachment.

3 Use a cover stitch or a chain stitch. Check your instruction manual for setup.

4 Lower the presser foot and take a few stitches by hand to secure the end. Keep fabric turned under as you sew and sew at a steady speed to roll the fabric consistently.

Create casings, elastic/ribbon and hems with this unique attachment by using various sizes ¼" to 1".

Feller attachment two-needle wide cover stitch

Feller attachment triple-needle cover stitch

chapter 4

Expand Your Knowledge

The projects in this chapter feature a span of complexity to help you gain confidence in your newfound skill—serging! Some projects are serged entirely, while others are completed in tandem with your sewing machine. Expand your knowledge of serging and explore new possibilities in our showcase of projects.

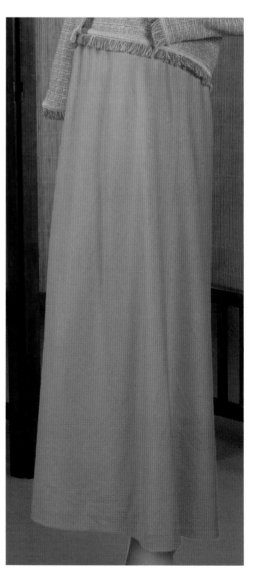

Serged Wardrobe

Serge a unique mix and match wardrobe featuring a stylish fringe trimmed jacket, linen bias-cut skirt, sheer print ruffled blouse, plus a coordinating handbag donned with decorative cover stitching. This wardrobe features many basic serger techniques, as well as several new and intriguing options. Check out the possibilities!

Sheer Print
Ruffled Tie Top

Begin your wardrobe with your favorite sheer retro print and make a ruffled blouse. Choose colors from the print for the remaining wardrobe components.

Instructions

1 Use a favorite blouse pattern designed for a sheer fabric.

2 Stitch inside seams with a 3-thread overlock and reinforce with a regular stitch on the sewing machine.

3 Finish outer edges of the hem, sleeves, collar and ruffle with a rolled edge.

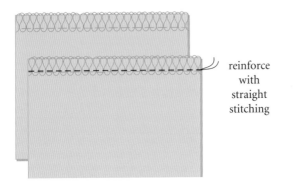

reinforce with straight stitching

Note from **Nancy**

Another serger seam option would be a 5-thread safety stitch—a chain stitch with a 3-thread overlock. (See page 52.) Check the instruction manual to see if this stitch is available on your serger.

4 Apply a liquid stabilizer such as PerfectSew™ Spray to the edges to be serged.

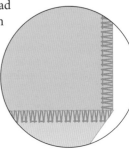

5 Set up the serger for a 2-thread rolled edge if it is available on your serger. Otherwise, use a 3-thread rolled edge. A 2-thread rolled edge is softer on sheer fabrics.

6 Use rayon thread in the needle and Woolly Nylon in the lower looper. (For a 3-thread stitch, use rayon in the upper looper, too.)

7 Use a normal width and a length of 0.5 mm to 1.5 mm (rolled setting).

Linen Bias-Cut Skirt

Team this versatile skirt with the fringe trim jacket and a knit top for a professional ensemble. Slip on a halter top and the sheer print blouse after a day at the office and you're ready to party!

Instructions

1 Use a favorite skirt pattern designed for linen fabric.

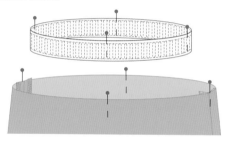

2 Stitch seams.
   - Use a straight stitch on a conventional sewing machine to stitch the seams.
   - Press seams open and edge finish with a 4-thread overlock.

3 Attach elastic.
   - Measure elastic equal to your waist measurement; subtract 3" to 4".
   - Cut elastic that measurement and stitch together to form a circle.

- Quarter elastic and quarter waistline. Mark with pins.
- Stretch elastic from one quarter-marking to the next. Serge elastic to the waistline edge using a 3- or 4-thread overlock with the longest stitch length.

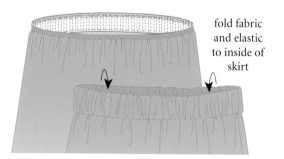

fold fabric and elastic to inside of skirt

- Fold fabric (including elastic) to the inside of the skirt to form the casing.
- Pin at quarter marks.
- Stretch from one pin to the next as you straight stitch in place with your sewing machine.

4 Complete the skirt.
   - Finish edge of the hem with a 4-thread overlock.
   - Hand stitch hem so the bias-cut skirt isn't stretched out of shape during the hemming process.

Cover Stitch Plaid Purse

This trendy purse, accented with a cover stitch plaid, goes from practical to chic. There's plenty of room for storage and an abundance of style!

Instructions

1   Use a favorite purse pattern. Cut the base fabric at least 2" larger on all sides than the pattern pieces.

2   Fuse interfacing to wrong sides of fabric before cutting out pattern pieces. A heavier interfacing, such as Pellon® ShirTailor®, is great for purses that require more stabilized sides.

3   Create a decorative plaid fabric using a cover stitch serger. (Check to make certain your serger can do a cover stitch and a chain stitch.)

- Mark an uneven grid on the interfaced side of the fabric, as shown above right, using the Chalk Cartridge Set. (The variety of chalk colors is perfect to designate the arrangement of your chosen thread colors.) For example: Mark all of the lines for a chain stitch in blue, all of the lines for a wide cover stitch in orange and all of the lines for a narrow cover stitch in green.

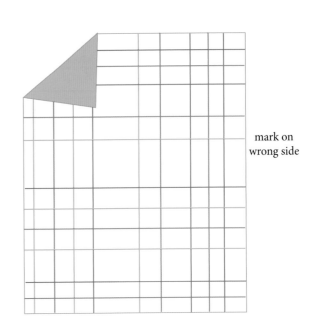

mark on wrong side

- Set up your cover stitch serger for a chain stitch.
  - Use decorative colored thread in the chain looper. (We used 12 wt. cotton thread.)
  - Use regular cone thread to match fabric in the needle.
  - Chain stitch on all blue lines with the marked interfacing side on top. (Looper chain is featured on the right side of the fabric.)

chain-stitched on blue lines

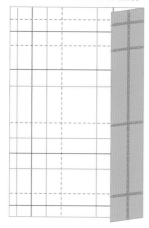

- Set up your cover stitch serger for a wide cover stitch (left and right cover stitch needles).
  - Use decorative thread in the chain looper. (We used a 12 wt. cotton thread.)
  - Use regular cone thread to match fabric in both needles.
  - Stitch a wide cover stitch on all orange lines with the marked interfacing side on top.
    (Looper chain is featured on the right side of the fabric.)

cover-stitched on orange lines

- Set up your cover stitch serger for a narrow cover stitch (center and right cover stitch needles).
  - Use decorative thread in the chain looper. (We used a 12 wt. cotton thread.)
  - Use regular cone thread to match fabric in both needles.
  - Stitch a narrow cover stitch on all green lines with the marked interfacing side on top. (Looper chain is featured on the right side of the fabric.)

cover-stitched on green lines

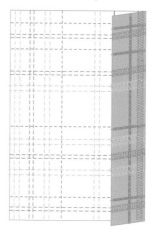

4   Cut out pattern pieces from the cover stitch plaid fabric and construct purse according to pattern instructions.

Cover Stitch Fringe Trim Jacket

You've seen it in ready-to-wear, but never dreamed it would be so easy to do on your serger! Choose your favorite jacket pattern or ready-made jacket and add this distinctive specialty trim.

Instructions

1 Decide where you would like to place the fringe trim on your jacket. We positioned it on the collar, cuffs and at the hemline.

2 Set up your cover stitch serger for a narrow cover stitch. (See page 47.)

3 See instructions on page 72 for creating the cover stitch fringe trim.

- Pin and baste trim in place on garment or other fabric accessory.
- Edgestitch trim in place with sewing machine.

Trendsetting Accessories

*Exquisite fabrics create these trendy, yet elegant, accessories. Complete them in no time with easy serger techniques. Perfect for presents—or give them to a deserving...**you!***

Supplies Needed
- ¼ yd. Fabric A (silk shantung—purse and carriers)
- ¼ yd. Fabric B (silk shantung—lining)
- Decorative thread such as Premium Sulky® 30 wt. cotton blendables (chain looper)
- All-purpose thread (needle)
- 1½ yd. purchased cording (handle) or make custom cording using your favorite technique
- Beads for tassels and embellishment, or purchased tassels

Serged Sonata Evening Bag

This clever evening bag is so charming it will put a song in your heart. The only thing going solo in this serged sonata is its unique style. Chain stitching on silk and an abundance of beautiful beads create a harmonious blend of techniques.

Instructions

1. Sketch the simple bag pattern (includes ¼" seam allowances).
   - Draw a 6¼" x 8½" rectangle on pattern paper. Cut out.
   - Fold in half lengthwise, meeting 8½" edges.
   - Measure up 3" from the bottom on the cut edge and mark.
   - Draw a line from the 3" mark to the fold at the center of the rectangle. Trim along this line through both layers.

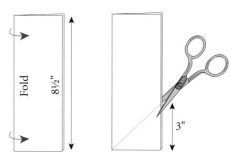

2. Prepare fabric.
   - Cut a 2½" crosswise strip (carrier) from Fabric A. Subcut one 2½" x 5" strip.

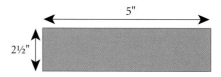

- Cut two bags from Fabric B (lining), using bag pattern.
- Cut one 8" x 18" rectangle Fabric A (purse).
- Mark a 45˚ angle on the wrong side of the 8" x 18" Fabric A rectangle (purse) starting at upper right corner.
- Draw additional lines parallel to the first line ¾" apart.

3   Set up the serger.
- Adjust serger for a chain stitch using center needle.
- Thread needle with all-purpose thread; use a decorative thread in the chain looper.

4   Serge along traced lines.
- Chain stitch along traced lines on the wrong side of the purse fabric.
- When chain stitching on the serger, always stitch off onto a piece of scrap fabric. This prevents the decorative thread from getting caught in the lower loopers.
- On the wrong side of the carrier strip, chain stitch ¾" from each 5" edge.

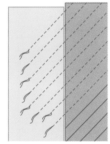

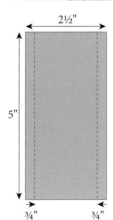

5   Cut bag sections.
- Cut two bag pattern pieces from the serged fabric, matching chain-stitched lines.

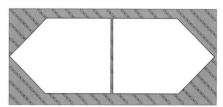

- Apply Fray Check™ to the cut ends of the chain stitching to prevent raveling.

6   Make and position tassel.
- Make a bead tassel using your favorite technique or use a purchased tassel.
- Position the tassel on the right side of one of the serged bag pieces, placing the knot at the cut edge of the bag point as shown. Baste in place.

7   Construct the bag using a ¼" seam allowance.
- Set up the serger for a 4-thread overlock stitch.
- Fold the 2½" x 5" carrier in half lengthwise, right sides together, and serge 5" edge with a ¼" seam.

- Turn carrier right side out, centering seam on back of carrier.
- Cut strip into two 2½" pieces.

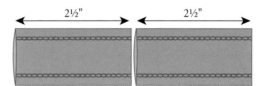

- Meet cut edges of each carrier.

- Position one carrier at upper right of one purse section, meeting right sides and cut edges, placing carrier 1" from top edge. Repeat, positioning remaining carrier at upper left. Baste in place.

- Meet purse sections right sides together, matching chain stitching at seamlines.
- Serge sides and lower edges of bag together, leaving the top open. Turn bag right side out.

- Repeat, meeting and serging side and lower edges of the lining, leaving an opening for turning the bag on one of the side seams.

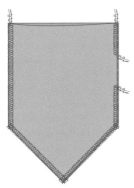

- Join the bag and the lining.
  - Slip bag inside lining, right sides together. Pin and serge upper edge, matching seams. Carefully remove pins as you serge.
  - Turn bag right side out. Hand stitch opening closed.

8 Complete bag.
  - Thread cord ends through carrier loops.
  - Decide on the final length of strap. Knot and hand stitch cording to inside edge of carriers.
  - Add bead trim to bottom edge of each carrier and bottom center of bag front, if desired.
  - Beads can also be stitched at random along corded strap, if desired.

Supplies Needed

- ½ yd. Fabric A (silk shantung—tote)
- ½ yd. Fabric B (silk shantung—tote accents)
- ½ yd. lining fabric
- ½ yd. batting
- Four spools variegated rayon thread (chain and cover stitch accents)
- Four spools regular two-ply cone thread

Chained Leaves Tote

Create this elegant tote with its chain and cover stitch accents. Use it as a tote or a roomy purse; either way, you'll find it difficult to leave at home!

Instructions

1 Prepare fabrics.
- Fabric A: Silk Shantung (tote):
  - Cut two 14" x 17" pieces (tote front and back).
  - Cut two 3" x 14" rectangles (handles).

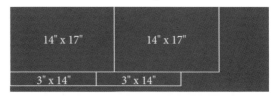

14" x 17"	14" x 17"
3" x 14"	3" x 14"

- Fabric B: Silk Shantung (tote accents)
  - Cut four 4" x 14" strips (accent panels).
  - Cut two 2" x 14" strips (flat piping for handles).
  - Cut one 1½" x 8" bias strip (loop).
  - Cut one 3" x 8" bias strip (button).

4" x 14"	4" x 14"
4" x 14"	4" x 14"
2" x 14"	
2" x 14"	1½" x 8" 3" x 8"

- Batting
  - Cut two 14" x 17" pieces (tote front and back).
  - Cut two 1½" x 14" rectangles (handles).
  - Cut one ¾" x 7½" rectangle (button).
- Lining
  - Cut two 14" x 17" pieces (tote front and back).
  - Cut one inside pocket to desired size using remaining lining fabric. Finish pocket edges using your favorite technique.

2 Quilt front and back of tote.
- Draw vertical chalk lines 1½" apart on lining.
- Layer fashion fabric, lining and batting.
  - Position Fabric A right side down.
  - Place batting over wrong side of Fabric A.
  - Position lining fabric over batting, right side up.
  - Pin all layers together.
- Set up serger for a chain stitch, following instruction manual. Use variegated rayon thread in both the needle and the chain looper.
- Chain stitch vertical rows on lining side of the layered fabric sandwich. Use an anchor cloth at the end of each row. (See page 46.)
- Draw freehand leaf designs on the wrong side of each accent panel. Chain stitch the designs.
- Add accent panels to the tote, right side up.
  - Press under ½" along each 14" side of accent panel.

- Place accent panels 3" in from each 14" edge of quilted tote front and back. Pin.
- Optional: This would be a good time to catch a finished inside pocket in place while securing the accent panels. Sides and bottom of a pocket may be caught in the tote seams.

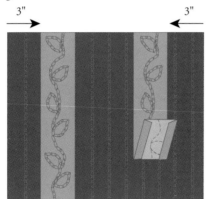

- Edgestitch panels with chain stitch to secure.
- Place front and back panels wrong side up and restitch, following the previous stitching lines so the decorative chain forms on the front side of tote.

3   Construct handles.
  • Use a chain stitch with variegated rayon thread in the needle and the chain looper.
  • Press the two 3" x 14" handles in half lengthwise, wrong sides together. Open up handles and press cut edges to center press marking. Press.
  • Unfold handles and center 1½" x 14" batting in the handles. Refold to enclose batting.
  • Meet 14" edges of flat piping, wrong sides together; press. Insert into handles, meeting raw edge of piping to center cut edge of handles; pin. Piping extends ¼" beyond handle edges.
  • Refold handles, enclosing piping. Edgestitch with chain stitch, following handle edges.

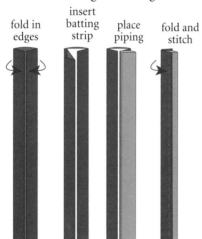

| fold in edges | insert batting strip | place piping | fold and stitch |

4   Construct loop.
  • Set up the serger for a triple cover stitch. (See page 49.) Use variegated rayon thread in needles and chain looper.
  • Press 1½" x 8" bias loop strip in half lengthwise. Unfold and press raw edges to center press mark.
  • Stitch down the center with a triple cover stitch.

5   Construct button.
  • Press 3" x 8" button strip in half lengthwise. Unfold strip and center batting. Press the short ends ¼" toward the wrong side, over the short ends of batting. Press both lengthwise raw edges to center. Press outside edges to center again. Stitch with a triple cover stitch centering stitching over center folded edges.

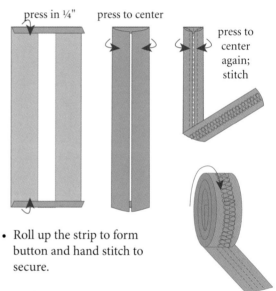

press in ¼"   press to center   press to center again; stitch

  • Roll up the strip to form button and hand stitch to secure.

6   Complete tote.
  • Pin handles to front and back, right sides together, aligning handles with inside edges of accent panels. Stitch ¼" from edge using a sewing machine to secure.

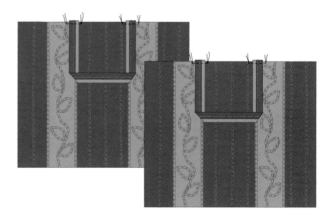

- Pin loop closure to center on back panel, right sides together. Stitch ¼" from edge.

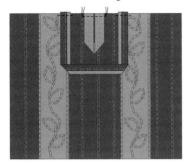

- Set the serger for a 4-thread overlock stitch using two-ply cone thread.
- Position right sides of front and back together. Serge the side seams and across the bottom with a 4-thread overlock. (Serge a ⅝" seam, trimming off excess fabric.)
- At bottom corners, meet side seam to bottom seam and pin so a triangular point forms.
- Measure 1½" down from corner and draw a chalk line.

- Shape the corner by stitching across the corner on chalk line with a sewing machine. Repeat for opposite corner.
- Turn tote right side out.
- Serge around top edge of tote through all thicknesses.
- Stitch ½" from the top edge of tote with a conventional machine, catching handles and loop in place.
- Press a ¾" hem to the inside, bringing handles and loop to the top of the tote.
- Topstitch top hem in place with a chain stitch, conventional machine straight stitch or hand stitch.
- Sew fabric button to front to correspond with loop.

Cover Stitch
Glamour Scarf

This exquisite organza and satin scarf features decorative rayon cover stitch highlights.

Supplies Needed
- ⅓ yd. organza (scarf)
- ¼ yd. satin (appliqué pieces)
- Three spools rayon thread
- Lightweight paper-backed fusible web

Instructions

1 Prepare fabric.
   - Cut a 10" crosswise strip of organza.
   - Back the wrong side of satin with a lightweight paper-backed fusible web.
   - Trace and cut four 2" squares and six 2" x 6" rectangles.

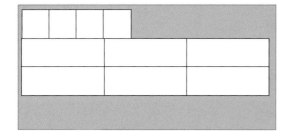

   - Remove the paper backing from the satin. Arrange squares and rectangles as shown. Position squares ½" from the short ends of the scarf to allow room for fringing the ends of the scarf.

- Fuse satin in place, covering it with a press cloth to avoid damaging the surface of the fabric.

2 Set up serger for a cover stitch, threading the chain looper, left needle and right needle with a decorative thread such as rayon embroidery thread. This thread adds luster without a lot of weight.

3 Serge over each edge of the satin with a cover stitch.

- Stitch from the underside of the fabric, positioning the cut edge of the satin in the center of the foot.
- Serge all lengthwise edges first.

- Serge crosswise edges.

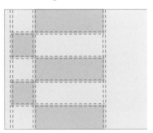

- Raise the needles, making sure they're at the highest position. Lift the presser foot; remove fabric from the serger by firmly grasping the fabric and pulling the threads to the back of the machine.
- Trim thread tails. Apply a drop of seam sealant to each end of the cover stitching.

4 Complete the scarf.
- Finish lengthwise edges of scarf with a rolled edge.
- Fringe the ½" section at each end of the scarf.

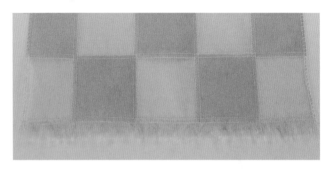

Flatlock
Patchwork Scarf

This stylish scarf, adapted from a design found in an exclusive boutique, features flatlocked satin and organza patchwork at each end.

Supplies Needed
- ½ yd. satin fabric
- ¼ yd. organza
- Rayon or all-purpose thread (needle)
- Decorative thread (lower looper)

Instructions

1   Prepare fabric: Cut two 2½"-wide crosswise strips of both organza and satin.

2   Set up serger.
- Adjust the serger for a narrow 2-thread flatlock.
- Attach the regular presser foot.
- Thread the right needle with rayon or all-purpose thread; use decorative thread in the lower looper.

3   Create the patchwork.
- Meet strips, wrong sides together, alternating fabrics. Flatlock strips, guiding fabrics about ⅛" away from the blade so none of the fabric is trimmed away. Loop stitches will be visible on the right sides of the fabrics.

- Flatten the strips; subcut them into 2½" sections.

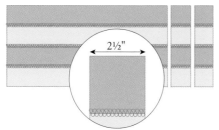

- Rotate alternate sections 180 degrees to form a patchwork design, meeting a satin section on one strip to a sheer section on the next. Join sections with flatlocking, right sides together. Ladder stitches will be visible on the right sides of the fabrics.
- Join as many sections as needed for each end of the scarf.

4   Complete the scarf.
- Cut a satin strip the same width as the patchwork and as long as desired. Flatlock a patchwork section to each end of the satin, right sides together.
- Serge around outer edges with an overlock or rolled edge to complete the scarf with decorative threads in the needle and lower looper.

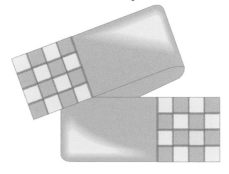

Supplies Needed
- ⅔ yd. organza
- Wash-away stabilizer
- 30- to 40-pound test fishing line
- Two spools all-purpose thread
- One spool decorative thread (such as metallic iridescent rayon thread)
- Elastic foot

Organza
Gift Wrap

When you need a wrap for a special gift consider using organza. Then use your serger and fishing line to add support and stability to the fabric's edge. It's an ideal finish for bridal veils or evening wear, too.

Instructions

1 Prepare fabric.
- Cut a circle of organza about 22" in diameter.
- Cut strips of wash-away stabilizer, such as Avalon by Madeira. Place them on top of the fabric edges while serging to eliminate the "pokies." A wider stitch width is also helpful.

Note from **Nancy**

Pokies are fibers that protrude from a rolled edge, especially on the crosswise grain or on ravel-prone fabrics.

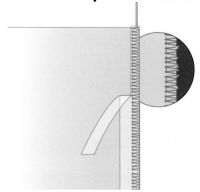

2 Set up serger.
- Attach a serger foot with a thread guide, such as an elastic foot. (See page 75.)
- Cut and insert the end of approximately 3 yards of fishing line into the thread guide of the specialty foot. If a specialty foot is not available, manually position the fishing line along the fabric edge.
- Set the serger for a 3-thread rolled edge using all-purpose thread in the needle and lower looper and a decorative thread such as a metallic iridescent rayon thread in the upper looper.

3 Serge along the edge of the organza.
- Trim off a small amount of fabric and encase the fishing line as you serge.
- Carefully tear away excess stabilizer after stitching is complete.
- Remove any remaining stabilizer by spritzing with water.

4 Place a gift in the center of the Organza Wrap and tie with a favorite ribbon.

Instructions

1 Prepare fabric.
- Cut fabric for the ribbon any width or length you choose. We used a 3½" x 45" strip of cotton fabric for our bow.
- Cut strips of wash-away stabilizer to place on top of the fabric edges while serging to eliminate "pokies."

2 Set up serger.
- Attach a serger foot with a thread guide, such as an elastic foot.
- Cut and insert the end of approximately 3 yards of 28-gauge wire into the thread guide of the foot. If a specialty foot is not available, manually position the wire along the fabric edge.
- Set the serger for a 3-thread rolled edge using all-purpose thread in the needle and lower looper and a decorative thread such as a metallic iridescent rayon thread in the upper looper. Set stitch length close enough so it covers the wire.

3 Serge along the edge of the fabric.
- Trim off a small amount of fabric and encase the wire as you serge.
- Carefully tear away excess stabilizer after stitching is complete.
- Remove any remaining stabilizer by spritzing with water.

Supplies Needed
- ⅛ yd. fabric
- 3 yd. 28-gauge wire
- Wash-away stabilizer
- Two spools all-purpose thread
- One spool decorative thread
- Elastic foot

Wire-Edged Ribbons

Imagine the possibilities and the savings when you create your own wire-edged ribbon. Coordinate fabrics, colors and choose your own width! It's fast and easy to do with a serger rolled edge, using a specialty foot to hold the wire.

See illustrations from the Organza Gift Bag, page 99, as the techniques for Wire-Edged Ribbons are similar.

Pillow Options

Sometimes the easiest items to create—the pillows—set the color scheme for an entire room! Many shapes and sizes with interesting fabrics, colors and textures are what a designer looks for. Art Deco to Americana—state your style with pillow options!

Rolled Edge
Flange Pillow

The magical flange is an easy technique with a spectacular look! When you team it with a rolled edge, this pillow is exceptionally easy to finish. Let the fabric make the statement on this classic accent.

Supplies Needed
- 14" pillow form
- ⅝ yd. fabric
- Decorative thread

Instructions

1 Prepare fabric.
- Cut two 19½" fabric squares.
- Mark 2" from all four cut edges on the right side of one 19½" square.
- Stack fabrics wrong sides together.

2 Construct pillow.
- Use a sewing machine to stitch along the marked lines on three sides of the pillow.
- Insert the pillow form.
- Stitch the remaining side closed along the marked line using a zipper foot.

3 Serge to complete the pillow.
- Set up the serger for a rolled edge with decorative thread in the upper looper.
- Serge around the pillow flange, catching both layers of fabric.

Cover Stitch Pintucks Pillow Sham

This creative endeavor pays off with a sophisticated new version of pintucks. It's a "knock out" addition to your pillow collection!

Supplies Needed
- Standard bed pillow
- 1¾ yd. lightweight cotton fabric
- ⅓ yd. Pellon® ShirTailor® interfacing
- Three cones serger thread

Instructions

1 Create pintucks.
- Use the full length and width of fabric to make pintucks. Mark diagonal lines 1½" apart in opposite directions on the right side of the fabric, creating a criss-cross pattern.

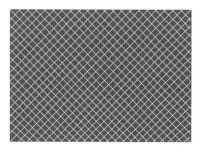

- Set up the serger for a right needle narrow cover stitch with a length of 3 to 4 and a standard width. Attach pintuck foot and a guide for making a pintuck without cording. (See page 78.) If you don't have the foot and guide or a cover stitch, use a rolled hem version of pintucks, as described on page 66.
- Serge pintucks on marked lines, working from the middle to each end. Repeat in opposite direction.

2 Complete pillow top.
- Cut a 30½" x 53" rectangle from the serged fabric.
- Press a 5" x 30½" strip of interfacing to the wrong side of each 30½" end and serge raw edge with a 3- or 4-thread overlock.

- Turn a 5" facing to the wrong side and topstitch in place with a sewing machine.

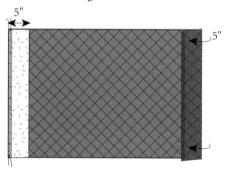

- With wrong side out, overlap faced edges to form a pillow 20" x 30½". Stitch side seams with a 4-thread overlock using ¼" seams.

overlap faced edges; stitch

- Turn right side out and insert pillow.

Deco 3-Thread Pillow

Use a 3-thread wide overlock with glossy Pearl Crown Rayon thread for stunning appeal.

Supplies Needed
- Two 8" squares faux suede
- Two spools Pearl Crown rayon thread
- One cone serger thread
- Fiberfill stuffing

Instructions

1 Mark ¾" from all four cut edges on the right side of one 8" square.

2 Stack fabrics wrong sides together. Use a sewing machine to stitch along the marked lines on three sides of the pillow.

3 Insert the stuffing.

4 Stitch the remaining side closed along the marked line using a zipper foot.

5 Serge edges of pillow.
- Set up a serger for a wide 3-thread overlock with Pearl Crown rayon thread in the upper and lower looper and cone serger thread in needle.
- Serge around the edges using one of the corner techniques on page 58.

Flatlock Duo Pillows

Serge a pair! This intriguing serger stitch is easy to do and with fabulous fabrics, you can express yourself ever-so-simply.

Instructions

1 Cut fabrics for your favorite size pillow.

2 Flatlock right side of pillow top.
- Set up the serger for a wide 3-thread flatlock.
- Use regular cone thread in the needle and lower looper and a decorative thread in the upper looper.
- Mark stitching lines on right side of fabric. Ours are about 2" apart, but use your creativity.
- Fold on marked lines and serge. Pull flat.
- Decorate with buttons if desired.

3 Complete pillow.
- Meet pillow front and back, right sides together.
- Serge pillow, leaving an opening for inserting fiberfill.
- Turn right side out. Insert stuffing. Hand stitch opening closed.

Supplies

- 4¾" x 7½" fabric strip (center)
- Two 6" x 24" fabric rectangles (side panels)
- Eight to 10 crosswise fabric strips (about 1 yd. total) Vary fabrics and strip width for an interesting appearance.
- 1½ yd. cording
- ¾ yd. fusible interfacing (22" wide)
- Seam sealant
- Bolster pillow
- Two coordinating 12 wt. cotton threads (loopers)
- One spool all-purpose thread (needle)

Wave Bolster Pillow

Here's a crazy patch bolster pillow with ingenuity! The wave stitch complements the vibrant silk fabrics and creates a trendy new serger version of crazy quilting!

Instructions

1 Set up the wave stitch serger for wide wave stitch. (See page 36. Stitch length 1.5; stitch width 5.0.)

2 Piece the pillow center.

Always place wrong sides together with pillow patchwork on top.

- Attach randomly selected strips to center, following numeric order below (log cabin rotation) until the diagonal measures about 16". Trim one set of opposite corners to "set" the chevron pattern and begin shaping a rectangle. Press and trim after each strip addition.

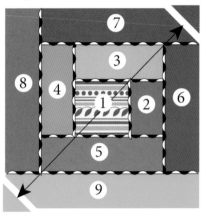

- Continue adding strips until patchwork rectangle measures approximately 16" x 27". When patchwork panel measures 27", trim points perpendicular to side edges.

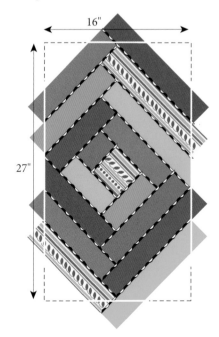

- Add strips to corners until they are filled out.

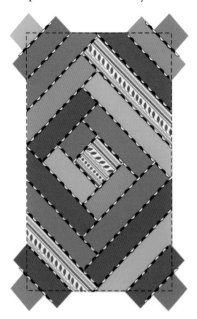

- After patchwork is complete, press the fusible interfacing to the wrong side of the pieced fabric rectangle. Trim the piece to 15" x 24". Dot seam sealant on any cut thread ends.

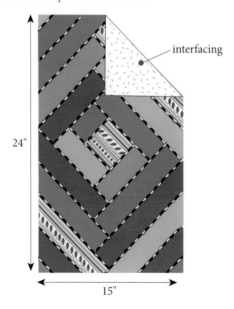

interfacing

24"

15"

3 Create bolster pillow sides.
- Stitch buttonholes into ends of each side panel.
  - Position both buttonholes 2" below long top edge of each panel, 1" in from each short edge.

- Stitch a buttonhole long enough to accommodate the ribbon or drawstring being used. (Generally, a ½"- or ⅝"-long buttonhole is sufficient.)

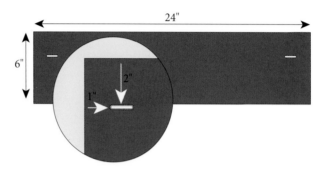

24"

6"

2"

1"

- Hem the long buttonhole edge of both panels.
  - Press under ½", then press under again 1" to form casing.

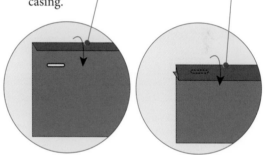

- Edgestitch in place. Buttonholes should be nearly centered between the fold and the stitching of the hem/casing.

4 Complete pillow.
- Placing wrong sides together and aligning 24" long edges, wave stitch side panels to each edge of patchwork center. (Remember to keep the patchwork on top.) Press seams.
- Serge the last seam, wrong sides together. Leave 5" tails at the beginning and end of the seam. Bury thread tails inside the seam using a double eyed needle.
- Insert cording or ribbon into casings. Insert bolster pillow form, tie and enjoy!

The Holiday Gathering

As the family gathers for the holiday, share this easy-to-serge home décor collection. The colorful patchwork tablecloth, napkins and basket centerpiece are destined to become your favorite techniques. Change the fabric and create a whole new collection for a perfectly coordinated party!

Party Patchwork Tablecloth

Create this festive tablecloth and set your table with holiday cheer! Serger highlights include 2-thread flatlock, 3-thread overlock and a simple chain stitch. A flannel backing eliminates the need for a table pad and keeps the tablecloth in place while you dine. Whether you're serving a candlelight dinner or showcasing a stunning centerpiece, this table topper is an elegant addition.

Supplies Needed
- 1⅝ yd. Fabric A (floral print)
- ¾ yd. Fabric B (red)
- ½ yd. Fabric C (green)
- ¼ yd. Fabric D (gold)
- 1⅝ yd. flannel backing (cream)
- Three spools 12 wt. cotton thread (gold)
- Two spools all-purpose sewing thread
- Seam sealant
- Sewer's Fix-it Tape
- Curved Basting Pins, size 1

Instructions

Flatlock all fabrics wrong sides together. After seaming, apply seam sealant to thread ends to prevent raveling.

1 Prepare fabric.
   - Fabric A (floral print): Cut six 9½"-wide crosswise strips. Subcut two strips into four 20" lengths.
   - Fabric B (red):
     - Cut one 7"-wide crosswise strip. Subcut into one 10" and two 15" lengths.
     - Cut five 3½"-wide crosswise strips. Subcut one strip in half for two approximately 20" lengths.
   - Fabric C (green):
     - Cut one 7"-wide crosswise strip. Subcut into one 15" and two 10" lengths.
     - Cut two 3½"-wide crosswise strips. Subcut one strip in half for two approximately 20" lengths.
   - Fabric D (gold): Cut two 3½"-wide crosswise strips. Subcut one strip in half for two approximately 20" lengths.

2 Set up serger for a 2-thread flatlock using 12 wt. thread in the looper and all-purpose thread in the needle.

3 Create the checkerboard center block.
   - Construct Strata 1.
     - Flatlock the two 7" x 15" Fabric B strips to opposite long edges of the 7" x 15" Fabric C strip.

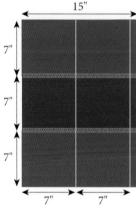

   - Open and press the pieced strip.
   - Subcut the strip into two 7" sections.
   - Construct Strata 2.
     - Flatlock the two 7" x 10" Fabric C strips to opposite long edges of the 7" x 10" Fabric B strip.
     - Open and press the pieced strip.
     - Trim the strip to 7".

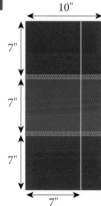

- Assemble the checkerboard.
  - Flatlock Strata 1 sections to opposite long edges of Strata 2 sections, making sure seams are aligned.
  - Open and press the pieced block.
  - Square the block to 20" x 20".

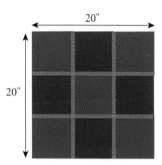

4 Create inner border corner blocks.
   - Construct Strata 3.
     - Flatlock two 3½"-wide Fabric B strips to opposite long edges of the 3½" wide Fabric D crosswise strip.
     - Open and press the pieced strip.
     - Subcut the strip into eight 3½" sections.

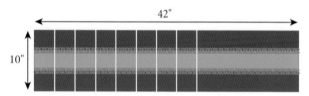

   - Construct Strata 4.
     - Flatlock the two 3½" x 20" Fabric D strips to opposite long edges of one 3½" x 20" Fabric B strip.
     - Open and press the pieced strip.
     - Subcut the strip into four 3½" sections.

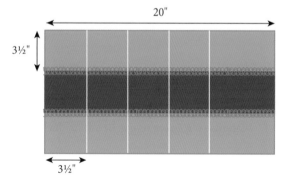

- Assemble the block.
  - Flatlock Strata 3 sections to opposite long edges of Strata 4 sections, making sure seams are aligned.
  - Open and press the pieced block.
  - Square the block to 9½" x 9½".

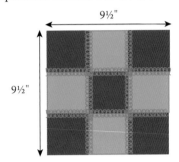

- Repeat, creating a total of four blocks.

5 Create outer border corner blocks.
  - Construct Strata 5.
    - Flatlock two 3½"-wide Fabric B strips to opposite long edges of the 3½"-wide Fabric C crosswise strip.
    - Open and press the pieced strip.
    - Subcut the strip into eight 3½" sections.

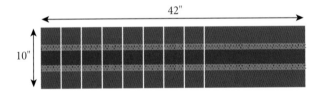

  - Construct Strata 6.
    - Flatlock the two 3½" x 20" Fabric C strips to opposite long edges of the remaining 3½" x 20" Fabric B strip.

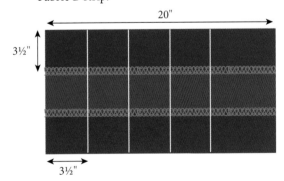

    - Open and press the pieced strip.
    - Subcut the strip into four 3½" sections.

- Assemble the block.
  - Flatlock Strata 5 sections to opposite long edges of Strata 6 sections, making sure seams are aligned.
  - Open and press the pieced block.
  - Square the block to 9½" x 9½".

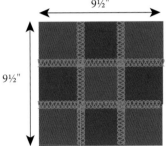

- Repeat, creating a total of four blocks.

6 Assemble the tablecloth top.
  - Attach inner borders.
    - Flatlock two 9½" x 20" Fabric A strips to left and right edges of the checkerboard center block.
    - Open and press the seams.

    - Flatlock inner border corner blocks to ends of the two remaining 9½" x 20" Fabric A strips.
    - Flatlock the pieced strips to top and bottom edges of the checkerboard center.
    - Open and press the seams.

- Attach outer borders.
  - Square up the tablecloth to 38" x 38". Trim the four 9½" wide crosswise strips to 38".
  - Flatlock a 9½" x 38" Fabric A strip to left and right edges of the tablecloth.

- Open and press the seams.

- Flatlock outer border corner blocks to ends of the two remaining 9½" x 38" Fabric A strips.
- Flatlock the pieced strips to top and bottom edges of the tablecloth.
- Open and press the seams.

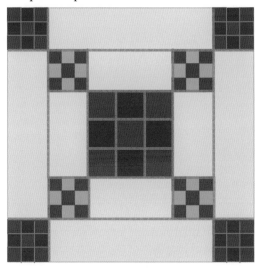

7 Layer, pin and quilt the tablecloth.
- Using a fabric marking pen, draw quilting guidelines extending from the tablecloth border seams to the outer edges. This creates a grid pattern for quilting.
  - Extend lines from the checkerboard center seams for optional quilting lines.
  - Extend lines from each end of the border seams.
- Place flannel backing right side down on a flat surface. Tape to surface with Sewer's Fix-it Tape.
- Position tablecloth right side up on top of the backing. Pin layers together using curved basting pins positioned at least ¾" away from the seams.
- Trim backing ½" beyond the tablecloth edges.
- Set up serger for a chain stitch as indicated in your owner's manual, using 12 wt. thread in the chain looper and all-purpose thread in the needle.

- Chain stitch slowly along the marked guidelines. If your serger does not chain stitch, use a conventional sewing machine to complete these rows of stitching. Stitch in the well of the seam to quilt the tablecloth.

8 Finish the outer edges of the tablecloth.
- Set up serger for a balanced 3-thread wide overlock stitch as indicated in your instruction manual.
- Square up and trim all edges even with the tablecloth top. Apply seam sealant to thread ends to prevent raveling.
- Chain 3" to 4" to provide a thread chain to hold onto at the beginning of stitching. Begin serging layers together at one corner.
- Stop stitching one stitch before the first corner. Using the hand wheel, bring needle out of the fabric to highest position, pull a little slack on the needle thread and pivot.
- Position corner just beyond position of needle, lower presser foot and continue stitching the following side.
- Repeat at the next two corners.
- At the final corner, pull starting tail under tablecloth and away from cutting blade.
- Serge off a 4"-long tail. Knot the tail close to the tablecloth edge.
- Using a double eyed needle, bury both thread tails within the overlock stitching on the underside of the tablecloth.
- Seal the corner with a dot or two of seam sealant for additional strength and ravel resistance.
- Attach one purchased tassel to each corner or create your own using 12 wt. cotton thread. (See page 73.)

Note from **Nancy**

Always keep fabric under the serger foot, as chain stitches need to be supported with fabric. Begin stitching on a fabric scrap (sometimes referred to as an anchor cloth); butt the tablecloth to the scrap and continue stitching. At the end of each row of stitching, stitch off onto the anchor cloth. Then clip the threads between the tablecloth and the anchor cloth. Reposition the tablecloth for the next line of stitching, with the edge of the backing next to the scrap that is under the serger foot. Stitch slowly, remembering to stitch onto the anchor cloth at the end of each row.

Supplies Needed
- ⅝ yd. cotton fabric
- ¼ yd. paper-backed fusible web
- ⅞ yd. Fast2Fuse™
- Three spools decorative thread
- 30-gauge wire
- Wire cutter
- 10" metal coat hanger

Holiday
Basket

Adapt this basket to fit the holiday or use it as a gift for any occasion. The decorative thread serging is simple and fun to do. Serge a wire-edged bow to adorn the basket. You'll want to make several for special gifts.

Instructions
1 Prepare fabric.
- Cotton fabric:
  - Cut two 12½" squares (base).
  - Cut two 2" x 30" strips (handle).
  - Cut two 2" x 20" strips (bow).
- Fast2Fuse™:
  - Cut one 12½" square (base).
  - Cut one 2" x 30" strip (handle).
- Fusible web: Cut two 2" strips and piece to make a 2" x 20" strip (bow).

2 Create basket base and handle.
- Layer the following:
  - One 12½" square cotton fabric, right side down
  - One 12½" square Fast2Fuse™
  - One 12½" square cotton fabric, right side up
- Fuse layers together, pressing the fabric to both sides of Fast2Fuse™. Trim to a 12" square.

Note from **Nancy**

Using an appliqué pressing sheet saves your ironing board from excess fusible as the layers are pressed together.

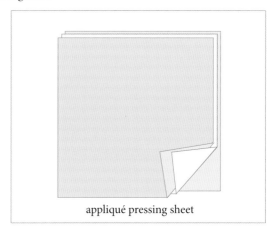

appliqué pressing sheet

- Layer and fuse the two 2" x 30" fabric and Fast2Fuse™ strips for the handle in the same manner. Trim to 1½" x 30".

3 Serge base of basket and handle.
- Set up the serger for a 3-thread overlock using 12 wt. cotton thread in the needle and the loopers.
- Serge around all four sides of base and handle. Finish ends with your favorite technique.

4 Create bow.
- Layer and fuse the two 2" x 20" strips of bow fabric and the fusible web, wrong sides together, following the directions on the fusible web.
- Set up serger with an elastic foot or beading foot. Place 30-gauge wire in the hole of the elastic foot or the groove in the beading foot. Disengage (lock) the cutting blade.
- Guide and serge the wire along the 20" edges of the bow fabric.
- To form the pointed tails on the ribbon, fold ends right sides together, aligning the edges. Stitch a ¼" seam across the ends with a sewing machine. Turn right side out.

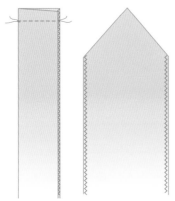

- Make a bow with the wire-edged fabric and secure the center with wire to shape.

5 Complete basket.
- Measure 3" from one end of the 30"-long handle section. Form a loop by bringing the serged end to the measured point. Stitch with a sewing machine to secure the end.

fold in
1½"

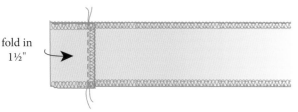

- Tuck the bow through the loop.
- Position the handle diagonally across the fabric base, with the bow 1½" down from corner and the handle extending past the opposite corner.
- Using a sewing machine, stitch the handle to the base, stitching next to the serged edge.
- Cut a 10" length of recycled coat hanger wire. Insert wire in the opening between handle and base. Bend the wire to shape the basket.

- Tuck free end of handle under bow. Hand stitch bow in place, covering the end of the handle.

Rolled Edge Napkins

Napkins are probably the simplest project to create on your serger. Make them any size—cocktail to full-size dinner napkins. Create a set for yourself or as a special gift.

Square Napkins

1 Cut the napkins to the size and shape desired. Common sizes to cut are 10", 15", 18" or 22".

2 Set up the serger for a 3-thread rolled edge using decorative thread in the upper looper if desired.

3 Use the Outside Corner method to finish the corners, as detailed on page 58.

Round Reversible Napkins

1 Cut two coordinating 17"- to 21"-diameter circles for each napkin. Use a yardstick compass if available.

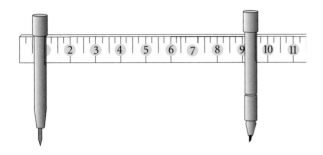

2 Apply glue stick or fusible spray to wrong sides of circles. Place circles wrong sides together.

3 Set up the serger for a 3-thread rolled edge, using decorative thread in the upper looper if desired. Or, use a narrow overlock hem with decorative thread such as 12 wt. cotton in the needle and loopers to finish edges. This edge finish is attractive on both sides.

4 Serge, using the Outside Circular Edge method on page 60.

5 To fold a round napkin into an elegant Christmas tree:

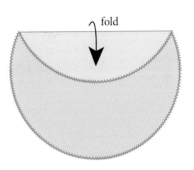

fold

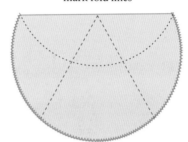

mark fold lines

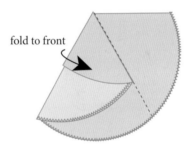

fold to front

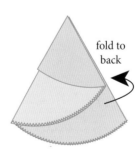

fold to back

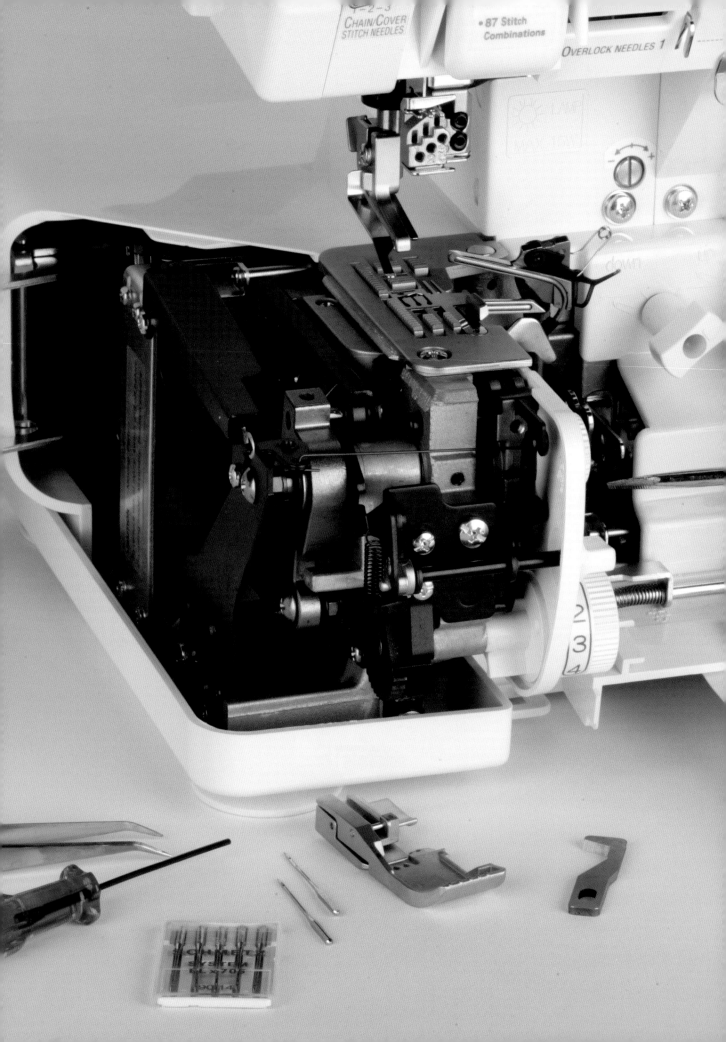

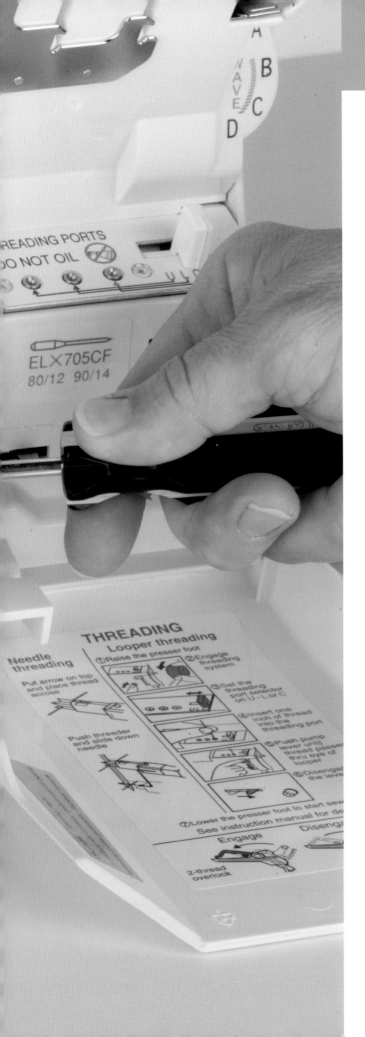

chapter 5

Serger Upkeep & Dilemmas

Don't call in the "handyman" to repair your serger. This finely tuned machine should be checked out by a trained specialist at least once a year. Regular care and basic maintenance will keep your serger (and you) humming along.

Serger Upkeep (Basic Maintenance)

Cleaning

- Clean the lint and trimmings from your machine after **each** project.
- Turn off the power to the machine before you do a thorough cleaning. Then remove the throat plate, disengage the blades and remove the presser foot.
- Loosen tensions completely and floss with a folded lightweight strip of fabric or unwaxed dental floss to remove broken threads and fibers.

- Use a stiff bristled brush, such as a small stencil brush, dipped very lightly in sewing machine oil to remove lint particles and gently lubricate the machine parts.
- Blow the dust from hard-to-reach areas of the serger using canned air. It may sound frivolous, but it works! Canned air is much better than blowing with your mouth, as canned air isn't moist. Another option might be to use a hair dryer on a cool setting. Take care that you don't blow lint into hard to reach areas of the serger.
- Keep your machine tidy and in good operating condition with a set of mini-vacuum attachments.
- Use 100% cotton balls as mini-dust mops to pick up the lint in your serger. Use a tweezers to hold the cotton balls for hard to reach areas. The lint clings to the cotton balls like a magnet!
- Use cotton swabs and a small amount of rubbing alcohol for cleaning the blade surfaces. When they are dry, apply a small amount of oil, wiping off any excess so it doesn't get on your fabric.
- Invest in a trim catcher for your serger. (See page 16.) The trim catcher prevents trimmed seam ends from falling in front of the serger or onto your lap.
- Purchase a small plastic maintenance tote for all your cleaning supplies, as it will keep them handy and ready to use. No excuses!

Note from Nancy

My favorite cleaner for the plastic outside casing of the serger is DK5. It removes any discolorations or residue certain fabrics may leave on the bed of a serger or sewing machine.

Needles

- Change your needles after three to five hours of serging.
- Leave the needle threaded when removing it from the serger. It's like a safety net; if it falls, it won't end up inside the serger!
- Replace needles if they are burred, blunt or bent. If your thread keeps breaking, check for burrs on the needle, as this is a common cause for thread breakage. A blunt needle typically puts runs and holes in a fabric.
- Use the correct type and size of needle for your project. Make sure to insert needles correctly. A needle inserter is very helpful. Position the flat side of the needle toward the back of the machine and the long groove down the front of the needle.
- Make sure the needle is pushed up securely into the needle bar. Some machines have a little window for you to view the placement.
- Tighten the needle screw securely so the needle doesn't fall out when you are serging. Tighten the screw that is not supporting a needle as well.
- Keep a new package of needles, needle inserter and screwdriver in your maintenance tote.

Changing the Light Bulb

- Turn off the power to the machine before you change the bulb!
- Be very careful if you have been using the serger, as the light may still be warm.
- Check your instruction manual for directions on changing your light bulb.
- Use the correct type of bulb. There are many different types.

Blades

- Check your manual before changing blades to get them positioned correctly and at the proper height or take the serger in to your dealer to have them changed.
- Clean lint and thread from between upper and lower blades for sharper cutting.

- Clean blades with a cotton swab dipped in alcohol; then use a drop of oil to lubricate.
- Check for nicks and worn spots on the blades, as they will affect the cutting ability.

Oiling

- **_Clean_** the serger before oiling.
- Oil the serger after every 12 to 15 hours of serging.
- Check your owner's manual for oiling instructions. Some sergers do not need oiling.

- Use the oil supplied with the serger or sewing machine oil, rather than household oil. Serger oil is lighter and more refined.
- Serge a few stitches on an absorbent cotton fabric after oiling to eliminate excess.

Serging Dilemmas

What to do if…

Serger doesn't start
- Make sure the machine is plugged in and turned on.
- Check to see that the covers are closed. As a safety feature, many sergers won't operate with the looper cover open.
- Remember to release the machine lock button if you have Jet-Air Threading™. The serger will make a humming noise and your machine will not start if the lock button is compressed.

Thread breaks
- Check the threading. Incorrect threading is the most common cause of stitching problems. Thread the serger in the proper sequence.
- Check the needles. Sometimes they are burred, which can cause thread to break.
- Use the correct needle and make certain it is fully inserted.
- Check that the tension is not too tight.
- See if one of the threads is caught on a spool notch, thread guide or thread stand.
- Use a good-quality thread.

Stitches skip
- Check the threading.
- Use the proper needle and needle size for the project. Make sure the needle is fully inserted.
- Check to see that your needle is not dull, burred or bent, any of those needle conditions can cause snagging and skipped stitches.
- Check to see that the thread is appropriate for the serger.
- Prewash fabric to remove any residue from the fabric finishing process.
- Adjust foot pressure. (See page 27.)
- Check thread for irregularities.

Fabric won't feed under the presser foot
- Check that the presser foot is lowered.
- Lengthen the stitches. If the stitch length is too short, the machine may jam.
- Lift the toe of the foot or the whole presser foot to start serging. This can help prevent threads from bunching up and feeding unevenly.
- Check blades for wear.
- Check your presser foot pressure. It may be too tight for lightweight fabrics or too loose for heavy fabrics.
- Clean lint out of feed dogs.

Stitches are not balanced
- Check threading.
- Check tension settings.
- Make sure thread is spooling off the cones correctly.
- Use the proper size needle.
- Check stitch dial (if you have one) to make sure it is set for the correct stitch symbol.
- Check looper threading.
  - Thread may be too thick.
  - Rethread following all guides. Thread the loopers and needles in proper sequence making sure loopers aren't crossed when threading.

Blades don't cut well
- Replace one or both blades if cutting is ragged and uneven. Test by stitching on a lighter-weight fabric.
- Check your instruction manual to properly change and position blades.
- If you have changed your blades and they still aren't cutting correctly, take the serger to your dealer. The blades may not be at the proper height.

Needle breaks
- Insert a new needle using your instruction manual as a guide.
- Loosen tension on the needle and upper looper threads.
- Use a larger size needle.
- Insert pins parallel to the edge and outside the presser foot area so the needle and cutter won't hit them.
- Avoid pulling on fabric while serging.
- Check thread guides for caught thread.

Fabric puckers
- Rethread.
- Loosen the needle tension.
- Shorten the stitch length.
- Adjust pressure on the foot.
- Adjust differential feed (if available on your serger).

Seams pull apart
- Tighten the needle tension or loosen the lower looper tension.
- Check that thread is engaged in tensions.
- Use a 4-thread overlock seam or reinforce seam with straight stitching. (See page 28.)

Tension Troubleshooting

Adjusting the tensions is probably the most important technique to learn about your serger. You may need to adjust the tensions with just about every change in stitch, fabric or thread type. New stitch variations are actually created by specific tension adjustments! This section will help you recognize balanced serger stitches—and show you how to adjust them if they aren't quite right. The illustrations in this section should help you in the process.

Tension Basics

- Check your instruction manual for tension adjustments on stitches available on your serger.
- If you have serger knobs, remember "righty tighty; lefty loosey." If you have lay-in discs or dials, turn them up to tighten and down to loosen.
- Make one adjustment at a time and then serge to see if the stitch quality has improved. Making too many adjustments at one time can be confusing!
- If a thread loops, too much thread is coming from the spool; tighten that tension. If threads pucker or draw in, too little thread is coming from the spool; loosen the tension.

Note from Nancy

Familiarize yourself with serger tension by using a different color of thread for each needle and looper. This will help you more accurately identify threads in a stitch.

Effects of Thread, Stitches and Fabric

- Loosen tensions for heavier fabrics, which need more thread for coverage.
- Tighten tensions for lighter-weight fabrics, which need less thread for coverage.
- Loosen tensions when using heavier threads, as they take up more space in the tension controls.
- Loosen tensions when using stretchy thread such as Woolly Nylon, as it stretches when it passes through the tension controls and threading guides.
- Adjusting the looper tension controls how much thread is released from the spool for various stitches. Loosen looper tensions for a longer or wider stitch; tighten looper tensions for a shorter or narrower stitch.

3/4-Thread Overlock Tension Adjustments

Balanced 3-Thread Overlock

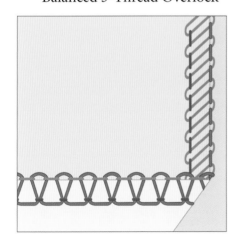

- ● left needle
- ● right needle
- ● upper looper
- ● lower looper

Balanced 4-Thread Overlock

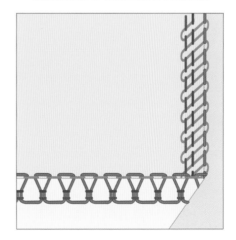

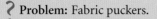

? Problem: Fabric puckers.

! Solution: Loosen the needle tension.

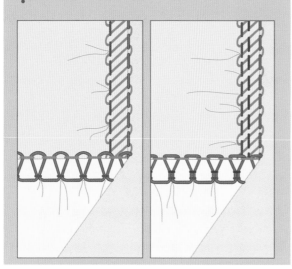

3-Thread Overlock
- ● left needle
- ● right needle

4-Thread Overlock
- ● upper looper
- ● lower looper

? Problem: Loops or V's form on the underside and seam may pull apart.

! Solution: Tighten the needle tension.

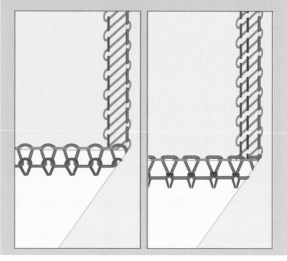

3-Thread Overlock
- ● left needle
- ● right needle

4-Thread Overlock
- ● upper looper
- ● lower looper

? Problem: Lower looper threads are pulled to the right side of the fabric.

! Solution: Loosen the upper looper tension, or tighten the lower looper tension.

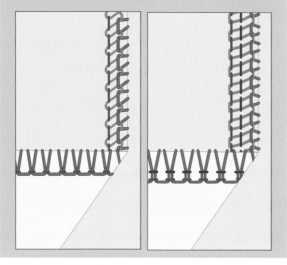

3-Thread Overlock
- ● left needle
- ● right needle

4-Thread Overlock
- ● upper looper
- ● lower looper

? Problem: Upper looper threads are pulled to the underside of the fabric.

! Solution: Tighten the upper looper tension, or loosen the lower looper tension.

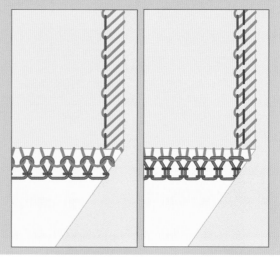

3-Thread Overlock
- ● left needle
- ● right needle

4-Thread Overlock
- ● upper looper
- ● lower looper

Chain Stitch Tension Adjustments

Balanced Chain Stitch

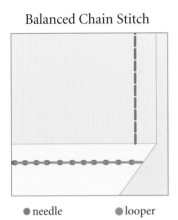

● needle   ● looper

? **Problem:** Pronounced loops on underside of the fabric.

! **Solution:** Loosen looper tension, or tighten needle tension.

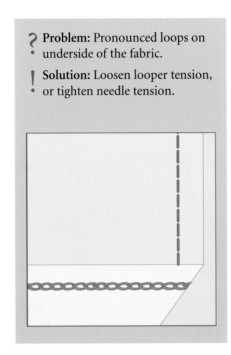

? **Problem:** Stitches break or won't form correctly.

! **Solution:** Loosen needle and/or looper tension. Lengthen stitches to 2.5 mm.

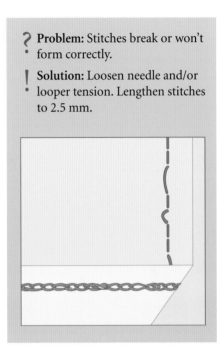

Cover Stitch Tension Adjustments

Balanced Cover Stitch

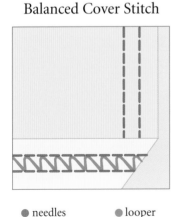

● needles   ● looper

? **Problem:** Fabric puckers.

! **Solution:** Loosen the needle tension, or tighten the looper tension.

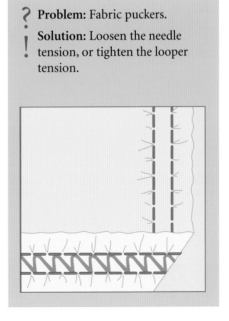

The stitches illustrated are a composite of 4- to 8-thread stitches. See pages 28 through 53 for specific stitches. If you have a 10-thread serger, check your instruction manual for tension adjustments that may be necessary for decorative stitches.

Tension Tidbits for Decorative Stitching

Decorative stitches are created by changing basic tensions, resulting in a stitch that is unique, yet functional. Rolled-edge and flatlock stitches are the most popular decorative stitches and the following information will guide you through adjusting the tension for these stitches.

3-Thread Flatlock Adjustment

- Start with a balanced 3-thread overlock stitch using the right needle. (See page 30.)
- Loosen the needle tension almost completely. It will form a V on the backside of the fabric.
- Tighten the lower looper tension almost completely. The lower looper will ride along the seam edge.
- Tighten or loosen upper looper tension slightly if necessary (depending on thread used). The upper looper will be on the top side of the fabric.
- Stitch on a folded edge or seam through two layers of fabric.
- For the best looking flatlock stitch, guide the fabric ⅛" to ¼" to the left of the upper blade so the stitches hang off the edge of the fabric. The stitches will lie flatter when pulled apart.

Balanced 3-Thread Flatlock

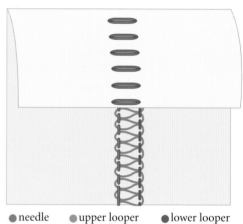

● needle　　● upper looper　　● lower looper

- If the stitch needs to be tighter and you have tightened the looper tension completely, use Woolly Nylon in the lower looper.

? Problem: Loopy, unstable flatlock.

! Solution: Tighten looper tensions.

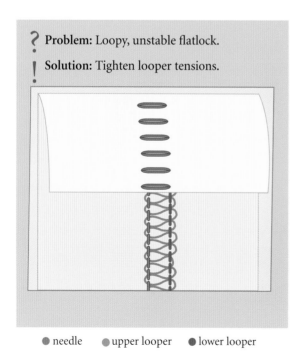

● needle　　● upper looper　　● lower looper

? Problem: Flatlock won't pull flat.

! Solution: Loosen needle tension.

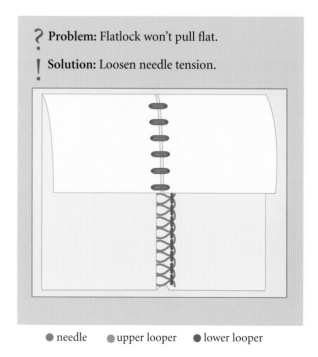

● needle　　● upper looper　　● lower looper

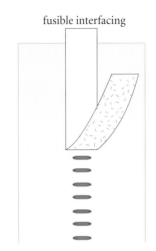

fusible interfacing

Note from **Nancy**

The most durable and best-looking flatlocks are achieved on knits. If you are flatlocking a woven and want to reinforce the stitching, press a strip of fusible knit interfacing over the seam on the wrong side.

2-Thread Overcast Tension Adjustments

A 2-thread overcast stitch does not lock at the seam, so it wouldn't be a good choice for constructing a seam. However, on a single layer of fabric, it is a great overcast stitch. The 2-thread overcast stitch is a "natural flatlock." When stitching two layers of fabric together, pull the fabric to flatten the stitch into a flatlock stitch.

Balanced 2-Thread Overcast

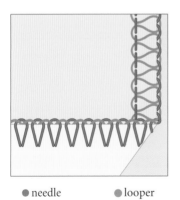

● needle   ● looper

? **Problem:** Looper threads are drawn around to under side of fabric.

! **Solution:** Loosen needle tension, or tighten looper tension.

? **Problem:** Needle threads drawn to right side of the fabric.

! **Solution:** Tighten needle tension, or loosen looper tension.

2-Thread Flatlock Adjustment

A 2-thread flatlock is less bulky and obviously uses one fewer spool of thread than a 3-thread flatlock. (It pulls flatter, so if you have this stitch available on your serger, use it instead of the 3-thread overlock. Check your instruction manual.)

- Start with a balanced 2-thread overcast stitch using the right or left needle, depending on the width you prefer. (See page 45.)

Balanced 2-Thread Flatlock

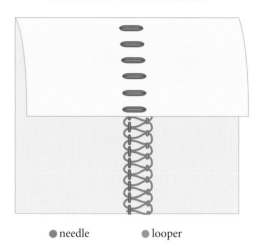

● needle   ● looper

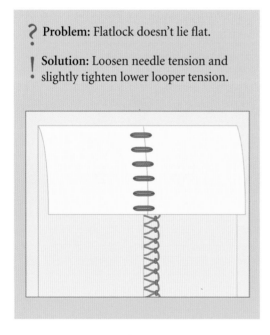

? **Problem:** Flatlock doesn't lie flat.

! **Solution:** Loosen needle tension and slightly tighten lower looper tension.

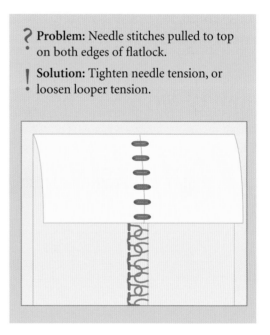

? **Problem:** Needle stitches pulled to top on both edges of flatlock.

! **Solution:** Tighten needle tension, or loosen looper tension.

- Tension adjustments usually are not necessary, as a 2-thread overcast does not lock at the seam. When the fabric is pulled it easily flattens.
- If the flatlocking doesn't lie flat, loosen the needle tension and slightly tighten the lower looper tension.
- For the best looking flatlock stitch, guide the fabric ⅛" to ¼" left of the upper blade so the stitches hang off the edge of the fabric.

3-Thread Rolled Edge Adjustment

- Change throat plate and/or presser foot, or possibly disengage the stitch finger, as necessary; check your instruction manual. You need a narrow stitch finger for a rolled edge. On some sergers, this adjustment is accomplished by the touch of a dial.

- Start with a balanced 3-thread overlock stitch using the right needle. (See page 30.)

- Tighten the lower looper tension almost completely. This pulls the upper looper thread around to the backside of the fabric. Test the stitch and tighten more as needed.

- Use Woolly Nylon in the lower looper.

- If you have tightened the lower looper as tight as possible and the rolled edge still isn't perfect, slightly loosen the upper looper tension.

- If the fabric puckers at the needle threads, loosen the needle tension.

- If the rolled edge pulls off the fabric edge, try wrapping the edge with a water-soluble stabilizer such as Wash-Away before serging.

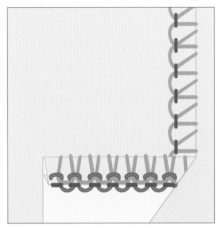

Balanced 3-Thread Rolled edge

● right needle
● upper looper
● lower looper

? Problem: Stitches do not roll completely to opposite side of fabric.

! Solution: Tighten needle tension, or loosen upper looper tension. Use Woolly Nylon in lower looper.

? Problem: Rolled edge pulls off fabric edge.

! Solution: Wrap edge with water soluble stabilizer. Widen stitch and/or lengthen stitch.

Refresh Your Memory

All-Purpose Thread: Standard weight three-ply parallel-wound thread generally used on a conventional sewing machine. Available in a greater range of colors than serger cone thread. Can be used on a serger, especially for decorative stitching to match a specific color.

Balanced Stitch: The ideal serger stitch in which upper looper, lower looper and needle tensions are adjusted so threads meet precisely at the fabric edge.

Binder Attachment: Specialty serger attachment used to attach bias binding strips to the edge of fabric. Available for single-fold and double-fold applications. Usually used with a chain or cover stitch.

Bite: The width of the stitch determined by the distance between the needle and the upper blade on a serger. It affects how much fabric is used to achieve the stitch.

Blades: Also referred to as "knives." The term refers to the cutting mechanisms featured on a serger. The upper blade moves up and down while the lower blade remains stationary for "scissors-like" trimming as you serge. Blades can be locked or disengaged so serging can be done without trimming the fabric.

Blanket Stitch: A finished edge that incorporates the 2- or 3-thread flatlock stitch, using decorative thread in a topstitching needle and a water-soluble stabilizer to pull the stitches over the edge of the fabric. Decorative thread forms "blanket" stitches on the right side of the fabric.

Blind Hem: A hemming procedure that hems and finishes the raw edge in one operation. Using a blind hem foot helps guide the fabric accurately as the serger hems the fabric. In an exemplary blind hem, the stitches are nearly invisible on the right side of the fabric.

Candlelight Thread: A decorative metallic thread designed specifically for the serger. Thread is cross-wound on cones so it winds off the spool with ease and has less possibility of tangling.

Chain Stitch: A stitch produced on a cover stitch serger when only one of the needles is used in conjunction with the chain looper. The top side of the stitch looks like that of a sewing machine, while the bottom forms a chain.

Cover Stitch: A stitch produced on a cover stitch serger using two or three needles in conjunction with the chain looper. The top side of the stitch looks like a sewing machine straight stitch using a double or triple needle, while the bottom forms a chain connecting two or three rows of stitching. An exceptional stitch for hemming knits, as the chain looper builds stretch into the seam.

Decorative Thread: Thread other than two-ply serger cone thread used to accent various stitches or to give them more depth.

Differential Feed: Two sets of feed dogs on a serger that are able to move independently. The front feed dog moves the fabric faster or slower than the back feed dog. Set to a larger number, it eases or gathers fabrics; set to a smaller number, it builds stretch into a seam.

Disengage Blade: Adjusting the blade to prevent the fabric from being trimmed when serging on a folded edge or serging beads or trim into position. On some machines, the blade is turned up and out of the way, while on others it is moved down and tightened or locked into position.

Double Eyed Needle: A hand-sewing needle with a large eye on each end. Useful for pulling the thread chain back through the overlocked edge.

Elastic Guide: A guide clipped or screwed to the bed of the serger and used in attaching elastic. Narrow elastic can be drawn through it and tightened with a screw-like mechanism, which forces the guide to tighten or loosen the grip on the elastic. Turn the screw clockwise to stretch the elastic and counterclockwise to decrease the stretch.

Feller Attachment: A specialty serger attachment that forces the fabric to turn to the reverse side for hemming, usually using a cover stitch or chain stitch. One to three needles form stitches on the topside of the fabric depending on the stitch used for hemming. The looper thread finishes the raw hem edge of the fabric.

Filler Cord: A heavier decorative thread or gimp used to serge between two layers of fabric to add the look of piping, as in corded pintucks. Also added for stability in a seam or for gathering.

Fishline Ruffles: An edge created by serging over a 30- to 40-pound test fishline with a narrow rolled edge. Ruffles using fishline will form a large lettuce-type edge when the opposite edge is gathered.

Flat Construction: Serging edges that will be seamed on a garment before construction so the seams can be traditionally sewn and pressed open. It is much easier to serge flat pattern pieces before construction.

Flatlocking: A serger stitch created by tightening the lower looper tension and loosening the needle tension on a 2- or 3-thread overlock. Serge a seam or the fold of a fabric; pull the two layers apart until the serging lies flat and it becomes a flatlock stitch. Upper threads form an overlock stitch, while the threads on the underside of the fabric form a ladder stitch.

Hemmer Attachment: A specialty serger attachment that turns under the cut edge of the fabric twice to finish the edge while it is serged with a chain stitch from the wrong side.

Jamming: A condition that occurs when thread wraps around the loopers and won't let the machine operate. Usually occurs when a serger is not threaded in the proper sequence. Gently trim the threads that are jammed together and rethread the serger in the right sequence, making sure the loopers are not crossed.

Jet-Air Threading™: An exclusive threading feature on many Baby Lock® sergers. One touch of a lever sends the thread through a tubular looper with a gust of air. The tubular loopers are engaged for threading and released for serging. Jet-Air Threading is used for upper, lower and chain stitch loopers.

Lettuce Edge: A rippled edge created by serging a short rolled or balanced stitch while stretching gently in front of and in back of the presser foot. Differential feed is usually set at a minus setting. Use on edges of stretchy knits, such as ribbing, interlock and Lycra®, or on bias-cut wovens.

Long Stitch: A serger stitch using a length setting of 4 mm to 5 mm.

Looper Threader: A tool with a long, pointed loop at one end used to simplify threading a serger looper. Thread is inserted through the loop and pulled back through the looper to finalize threading.

Loopers: Large-eyed metal parts within a serger, used to control the overlocking stitches. Sergers have an upper looper, a lower looper and (on some models) a chain looper.

Machine Lock Button: Button exclusive to the Baby Lock® machines. Used to engage the tubular loopers for Jet-Air Threading™.

Medium-Length Stitch: A stitch length of about 3 mm. Equivalent to about 10 stitches per inch, it is ideal for seaming most fabrics.

Medium-Width Stitch: A stitch width of about 3.5 mm from the right needle or 6 mm from the left needle. Measured from the left needle, it would be equivalent to a ¼" seam.

Overcasting: The process of finishing a raw edge of fabric by stitching on the serger with a 3- or 4-thread overlock and trimming the edge as you serge.

Overlocking: Using a 3- or 4-thread serger to overcast an edge. The loopers and needle(s) are used to "knit" the threads together on the edge of the fabric.

Pearl Crown Rayon: A heavy cross-wound rayon thread used in the loopers of a serger for a decorative edge. The sheen and thickness of this thread create an attractive overcast edge.

Pintucks: Small decorative folds in a fabric that are sewn or serged in multiples for a decorative effect. Achieved on a serger using a rolled-edge or narrow cover stitch.

Piping: A folded fabric strip with cording inside used to add interest and dimension.

Piping Foot: Aids in preparing a piping strip because the groove in the bottom of the foot helps it glide over the piping as it is stitched in place, close to the cording. Also allows you to make and attach piping in one step.

Presser Foot: The attachment for a serger or sewing machine that holds the fabric in place as you serge or sew. The edge of a presser foot is also used as a stitching guide to create a straighter seam.

Pressure Control: A screw or knob usually located on the top of a serger to increase or decrease pressure of the presser foot while serging. Turn clockwise to exert more pressure; counterclockwise for less pressure. Use more pressure on lightweight fabrics and less on heavy fabrics or stretchy knits.

Regular Cone Thread: A two-ply, cross-wound cone thread. Regular cone thread is finer and not as bulky when used in the interlocking loopers and needle threads of a serger.

Release Lever: A lever specific to the Baby Lock® serger with Jet-Air Threading™ that releases the machine lock button, opening the tubular loopers so the thread flows freely through the loopers as you serge.

Rolled Edge: the narrowest 2- or 3-thread stitch. Created by loosening the needle thread and tightening the lower looper for a 3-thread rolled edge. When the lower looper thread is tightened, it wraps the upper looper thread around the edge of the fabric. For a 2-thread rolled edge, the needle thread is tightened and the lower looper tension is loosened, wrapping the lower looper around the edge of the fabric. A 2-Thread Converter is necessary for a 2-thread rolled edge.

Safety Stitch: Also referred to as a back-up stitch. An additional stitch sewn with one of the needle threads (the fourth thread in a 3/4-thread stitch or the chain stitch in a 5- or 6-thread stitch).

Scalloped Edging: A decorative stitch achieved by serging a narrow 3-thread overlock and then stitching over it with a mirrored blind hem on a conventional sewing machine. It forms a scalloped edge—a nice finish on the edge of a lightweight project such as a receiving blanket.

Seam Finish: A stitching method used to prevent the edges of a seam from raveling. Examples include overcasting or overlocking the edge.

Seam Sealant: A product such as Fray Check™ or FrayBlock™ used to seal thread ends to keep a seam from unraveling.

Serger Patchwork: Using the serger to sew pieces or stratas together for quilting.

Serger Piping: Piping created with thread by serging a rolled edge on bias-cut tricot. Using a decorative thread gives more definition to the piping.

Stitch Finger: A small metal prong on the presser foot or throat plate. The stitches form on this prong when serging.

Thread Chain: The chain formed by overlocked threads in back of the presser foot when serging with no fabric underneath.

Thread Net: A mesh plastic net used to cover serger cones and spools during serging to prevent the thread from coming off too fast and pooling around the spools. It is especially helpful when using slippery threads such as rayon.

Tubular Loopers: Tubular loopers specific to Baby Lock® machines with Jet-Air Threading™. When the loopers are closed for threading, they form a tube to the eye of the looper, making threading easier and preventing threads from tangling.

2-Thread Converter: A spring-type mechanism that fits in a small hole at the top of the upper looper. It "tricks" the upper looper into thinking it is threaded so two threads (needle and lower looper) can be used for a specific stitch. Also referred to as "auxiliary looper" and "subsidiary looper."

Wave Stitch: A decorative 3-thread overlock serger stitch exclusive to Baby Lock® sergers in which the upper looper thread is alternately pulled and released while serging to form a wavy stitch.

Wide Stitch: A stitch length of approximately 7.5 mm from the left needle or 5 mm from the right needle.

Woolly Nylon: A texturized nylon thread. When pulled, it looks like regular thread; when allowed to relax, it "fluffs up" or fills in the stitches.

Wrapped Corners: A technique developed by Nancy Zieman to get sharp points on collars and other corners. Instead of stitching or serging around a corner in a continuous motion, one edge is serged first and then wrapped or folded toward the next corner before continuing to serge.